Dr. Robert Fyall is Old Testament tutor at St John's College, Durham, England. He is a graduate of the universities of St Andrews, Dundee and Edinburgh. In addition to his college duties, he is committed to a preaching and teaching ministry, being especially involved in Christian unions. For Christian Focus, he has also written *How God Treats His Friends*, a study of the Book of Job, and is currently writing a commentary on 1 and 2 Kings.

To
Carmen and Drummond

DANIEL

Robert Fyall

Christian Focus

© Robert Fyall
ISBN 1 85792 249 2

Published in 1998
by
Christian Focus Publications,
Geanies House, Fearn, Ross-shire,
IV20 1TW, Great Britain.
Cover design by Donna Macleod

Contents

Preface

It is difficult to remember a time when I have not loved the book of Daniel. Childhood memories of the Blazing Furnace and the Lion's Den in a large illustrated book of Bible stories are still vivid. From the same time I remember a book with illustrations of the beasts of Chapter 7 and the ram and goat of Chapter 8. I'm sure that at that time I had no idea of their connection with the earlier stories.

In more recent years Daniel has often been part of my regular preaching and teaching. I have preached through a large part of the book in my ministry at Claypath United Reformed Church in Durham. In lectures and conferences it has been a subject to which I have turned often.

However, I am particularly grateful again to Christian Focus for the invitation to write this commentary and to Malcolm Maclean for his shrewd comments and kindly encouragement. Writing a commentary forces consideration of passages hitherto neglected and gives a deeper perception of the whole book. I have thoroughly enjoyed this project and I'm glad to say now love the book of Daniel more than ever.

What I have tried to do in this commentary is to engage with a wide range of Daniel scholarship and make the results of this available to readers. Often I have referred to other commentaries and studies. Readers who do not have access to these nor time to consult them should not be put off. These are simply places where people who want to explore matters further can look. The aim of this commentary is to help people to love and understand this part of the Bible better. I hope it will also help preachers and teachers in their task of expounding Scripture as God's word for today. No one can write a commentary without drawing heavily on those who have done so before them. In the footnotes and bibliography I have acknowledged those writers who have particularly stimulated my thinking. If I have unwittingly echoed something without acknowledgement I apologise.

Books are not written in a vacuum and I am happy to thank a number of people. I am grateful to David Day, Principal of St. John's College, and the College Council for a term's study leave in the early part of which I finished this project. Once again I am indebted to Marianne Young of the secretarial staff of St. John's College who with characteristic efficiency and cheerful good humour put the whole manuscript on the word processor. To many students of the college who attended a recent series of Bible studies on Daniel and made many useful comments my thanks as well.

As always, this book could not have been written without the love and encouragement of my family. My wife Thelma has believed in, prayed for and helped forward this project from the beginning. I want to dedicate the book to my children Carmen and Drummond with the prayer that as they face the bewildering world of early teens they will grow up to be 'people who know their God'.

Selected Bibliography

Many books have been consulted but I have included here only those to which I have referred regularly. I have added a short comment on each; these are simply one person's opinion. Including a book does not necessarily imply approval of its stance:

Baldwin, J. G., *Daniel*, Tyndale Old Testament Commentary, IVP, 1978; perhaps the best conservative commentary; learned; sensitive and theological.

Calvin, J., *Commentaries on the book of the prophet Daniel*; Translated by Thomas Myers. 2 Vols. 1852-53; a classic exposition by the great Reformer.

Collins, J. J., *A Commentary on the book of Daniel*, Augsburg Fortress, 1993; sceptical, but encyclopaedic in its information.

Ferguson, S. B., *Daniel*, The Communicator's Commentary, 1988; a splendidly robust theological commentary.

Goldingay, J., *Daniel*, Word Biblical Commentary, 1989; accepts 2nd century date but a great deal of good theological reflection.

Hartmann, L. T. & Di Lella A. A., *The Book of Daniel,* Anchor Bible 23, 1978; useful on historical background.

Montgomery, J. A., *A Critical and Exegetical Commentary in the Book of Daniel,* I.C.C. 1927; old, but indispensable for serious study of the Hebrew and Aramaic text.

Philip, J., *By the Rivers of Babylon: Studies in the book of Daniel*, Didasko Press, a fine series of expository sermons by a distinguished pastor.

Porteous, N. W., *Daniel,* Old Testament Library revd. ed. 1979; fine theological work.

Russell, D. S., *Daniel*, Daily Study Bible, 1981; useful, but misses some dimensions by insisting on 2nd century date.

Wallace, R. S., *The Lord is King: The Message of Daniel*, IVP, 1979; useful exposition.

Young, E. J., *The Prophecy of Daniel*, Eerdmans, 1949; sober conservative exegesis.

Some important Dates

BABYLON
605: Rise of Nebuchadnezzar – Some Jews taken to Babylon (including Daniel, see 1:1).
597: 1st Siege of Jerusalem – Zedekiah made king by Nebuchadnezzar.
587: Fall of Jerusalem – Exile begins.
539: Fall of Babylon.

PERSIA
539: Cyrus allows Jews to return.
486: Xerxes 1 (Ahasuerus of 'Esther').
331: Darius III.

GREECE
334-331:   Alexander the Great conquers the Persian Empire.
323:       Death of Alexander – empire divided into 4 –
           The Ptolemies in Egypt ('the kings of the South' –
           Ch. 11) and The Seleucids in Syria ('the kings of
           the North') predominant.
175-164:   Antiochus Epiphanes.
167:       'The Abomination of Desolation' – i.e. altar to Zeus
           in the Temple.
165-164:   Victories of Judas Maccabaeus and cleansing of
           Temple.

For further dates and details of this period see commentary on Chapter 11. One other significant factor is the rise of Rome – in 168 Antiochus expelled from Egypt by Roman consul (see Dan. 11:30).

Introduction

The book of Daniel is usually either loved or loathed. The very qualities which make it so exciting to some, its vivid stories, dreams and visions, the colourful imagery and its apocalyptic messages prove uncongenial to others. A number of questions have to be examined so that we can be in a position to approach the book responsibly.

1. The Significance of the Exile

The book is set during that great disaster and watershed in Israel's history known as the Exile. A few words on the historical events will set this in perspective. After the death of Solomon his kingdom was torn apart, with the northern tribes (usually simply called Israel) eventually having Samaria as their capital. A rapid departure from obeying the Law of Moses followed and the kingdom was eventually destroyed by the Assyrians in 721 BC and many of the people deported to Assyria. The southern kingdom, centred on Jerusalem, remained. Much of the time apostasy prevailed there as well, although two great reforming kings, Hezekiah and Josiah, made valiant attempts to stop the rot.

Meanwhile the world scene was changing. The great Assyrian Empire was crumbling and in 612 its capital city Nineveh fell to the new and vigorous Babylonian state (an event celebrated by the prophet Nahum). In 605, Nebuchadnezzar came to the throne of Babylon, having smashed the power of Egypt. Jehoiakim, king of Judah (Dan. 1:1; 2 Kgs. 24:1) became his vassal. At this time there was probably no major devastation of the city, but some of the Temple vessels were taken, as well as some of the aristocracy, including Daniel and his friends. What happened next is not entirely clear, but Jehoiakim rebelled in 597 (2 Kings 24:1) and was succeeded by his son Jehoiachin who reigned a mere three months. Nebuchadnezzar returned and took the king and most of the leaders and professional class[1] to Babylon (2 Kings 24:1 ff.). He then installed Zedekiah as a puppet king; he rebelled towards the end of 598; then in 587 Jerusalem fell to Nebuchadnezzar and there was mass deportation and the Exile proper had begun.[2]

This shattering event called into question the whole basis of Israel's faith. The very centre of their belief was that Yahweh their God was the Creator and the Lord of history who had shown his power at the Exodus. Indeed that had not just been the defeat of Pharaoh and the Egyptian Empire. Rather Exodus saw it as the God of Israel defeating and destroying the gods of Egypt: 'I will bring judgment on all the gods of Egypt. I am the LORD' (Exod. 12:12). He had defeated Osiris and Amun-Ra; did the Exile mean that he was weaker than Bel and Nebo (see Isa. 46:1)?

What had happened to the Covenant? That bond made with Moses and then with David in such words as 'my love will never be taken away from him' (2 Sam. 7:15); where was that now?

What about the land 'that the LORD swore he would give to your fathers' (Deut. 1:8)? Jerusalem, 'Zion, the city of the Great King' (Ps. 48:2), that had gone as well. In any case in contrast with the brilliant culture of Babylon, Jerusalem must have seemed an insignificant backwater. 'How like a widow is she, who was once great among the nations' (Lam. 1:1) and 'How can we sing the songs of the LORD while in a foreign land?' (Ps. 137:4) are only two of the questions which echo through the later books of the Old Testament.

These are the huge questions which the book of Daniel grapples with and often we will return to these in the course of the exposition. Since Daniel's story starts at the very beginning of the Exile and goes on to its end and indeed a few years beyond that, the book gives a unique window into the entire period from an insider's point of view.

---

[1] One of those deported was Ezekiel and chapters 1-24 of his prophecy warn that Jerusalem is doomed. Only after the final fall of the city can he begin to preach a message of hope beyond the desolation.

[2] For further details on history see *Notes on Some Problems in the Book of Daniel*, D. J. Wiseman (Tyndale 1965); see also Baldwin pp 17-21.

However, much of the book, especially chapters 8-12, focuses on a later period i.e. the years following 175 BC when the Syrian king Antiochus IV intervened in the affairs of Palestine. Once again a brief summary of events will be useful. By the end of Daniel, the Babylonian empire had already been replaced by the Persian in 539. This in turn fell to Alexander the Great in 331 and he established a Greek empire. Upon his death however in 323, the empire split into four, each part seized by one of his generals. The predominant kingdoms were the Egyptian (the Ptolemies) and the Syrian (Seleucids). The Seleucid ruler who was most significant for the Jewish nation was Antiochus IV (Epiphanes) (175-164). He introduced a vigorous policy of Hellenisation. The whole culture, lifestyle and customs were to conform to Greek models. He had his nominee, Joshua, appointed as High Priest and given the name Jason. A Greek school was established in Jerusalem. Furious intrigues and infighting resulted in the establishment of Syrian troops in the city and the death penalty for practising the Jewish religion. The ultimate sacrilege ('the abomination that causes desolation', 9:27 etc.) occurred in 167. Antiochus erected an altar to Zeus on the altar of burnt offering and sacrificed pig's flesh on it. A new and worse exile had happened; not Jerusalem defeated by Babylon, but Babylon infiltrating Jerusalem.

However, at this moment determined resistance broke out under the great Judas Maccabaeus who, in a series of guerrilla campaigns and smashing victories, routed the Syrian armies and in 165-164 entered Jerusalem. The Temple was purified and dedicated, an event celebrated in the Hanukkah festival. See the commentary on Chapters 8-11 for further details on this period. Readers of Daniel should also read 1 and 2 Maccabees for essential background.

The book's perspective, then, stretches from 605 to 164, with a heavy emphasis on the later period in the second part of the book. The reasons for this will be examined in the relevant chapters of the commentary, but they give rise to some problems to which we now turn.

2. When and why the book was written?

The concentration on the Maccabaean period as well as historical difficulties in the first part of the book has led most modern scholars to dispute the traditional view that Daniel was written in the Exile and to see it instead as originating in Palestine in Maccabaean times. There are three main issues:

a. Historical

i. *Daniel 1:1*: It is argued that no siege of Jerusalem took place in the third year of Jehoiakim. However the verb 'besieged' may simply mean a show of strength and this fits well with 2 Kings 24:1 that Jehoiakim became Nebuchadnezzar's vassal. Moreover we know of Nebuchadnezzar's wars with Neco, the Pharaoh, who had put Jehoiakim on the throne of Judah.

ii. *Belshazzar (Chapter 5)*: This account is held to be fictitious because Belshazzar (Bel-šar-usur in the Babylonian texts) is not listed as king but only as crown prince, son of Nabonidus, last king of Babylon. However, Nabonidus was absent from Babylon for a decade during which he 'entrusted the kingship' to Belshazzar. Thus to argue that our author is inaccurate in calling him 'king' is splitting hairs. Moreover, the fascinating little detail of how the interpreter of the writing on the wall would become 'third ruler' (5:7, 16, 29) shows an understanding that Belshazzar was second to Nabonidus. Similarly he was not strictly 'son' of Nebuchadnezzar, but frequently in the Old Testament 'son' is used in a broader sense – e.g. 2 Kings 2:12 Elisha calls Elijah 'father'.

iii. *Darius the Mede (5:30 and 6:28)*: It is well known that Cyrus was the first ruler of the Persian empire and indeed the agent for the ending of the Jewish exile (see 2 Chr. 36:22-23; Ezra 1; and Isaiah 45:1). However we meet the mysterious figure of Darius the Mede in Chapters 5 and 6, and again in 9. The author is, of course, well aware of Cyrus (1:21; 10:1). Two considerations have been advanced. Darius has been identified with one Gubaru or Gobyras who was temporary governor of Babylon for Cyrus. The other is that Darius is, in fact, an alternative name for Cyrus himself. This would mean that 'and' in 6:28 would be an explanatory particle – 'the reign of Darius, that is, 'the reign of Cyrus'. A close parallel can be found in 1 Chronicles 5:26: 'So the God of Israel stirred up the spirit of Pul king of Assyria (that is, Tiglath-Pileser king of Assyria).' 'Pul' was the personal name of the army officer who on seizing the Assyrian crown took the throne name of Tiglath Pileser. This does not prove the identification of Cyrus and Darius but it does show that it is a consideration which should not be dismissed.

Readers who want to follow these matters further should consult the works by Wiseman and Baldwin already mentioned.

b. Linguistic
The book is written in two languages: Hebrew (1:1-2:4a; 8:1-12:13) and Aramaic (2:4b-7:28). The Aramaic section may (although this cannot be proved) have been circulated separately because of its more universal focus. Much controversy has centred around the Aramaic section and what it reveals about the probable dating of the book. Detailed discussion is not appropriate in a commentary of this kind,[3] but it should be remembered that since Aramaic became the international language in the Ancient Near East it exists in many regional, dialectical and cultural forms. Moreover, even the existence of Greek loan words is indecisive because Greek trading and cultural links with the eastern Empires is known from as early as the eighth century BC. There are no grounds for dating the book early on linguistics alone.

c. Theological
This is the main issue. The historical and linguistic matters have been and continue to be debated with impressive scholarship on both sides.

---

[3]Readers who know Aramaic should study 'The Aramaic of Daniel' by K. A. Kitchen in the symposium, ed. Wiseman mentioned above (pp. 31-79).

More fundamentally, could God reveal to a sixth century prophet events four centuries distant and, if so, why should he do so? The issues at stake are the trustworthiness of Scripture, the nature of God and the place of revelation.

The trustworthiness of Scripture is particularly emphasised in Chapter 9 where the ending of the Exile is specifically related to Scripture, especially Jeremiah in this case. Moreover, as we shall see in the exposition of that chapter, the prayer of Daniel draws heavily on earlier Scriptures. The book is not a freak intruder in the canon; it has its distinctive emphases, but is also integrated with the whole unfolding message of the Bible.

The God of Daniel is the God 'who reveals mysteries' and shows 'what will happen in the days to come' (2:28). This is so fundamental to the message of the book that to regard it as essentially a pseudonymous work of the second century tends to destroy the reader's confidence in the power of this God. If this God chooses to reveal part of the future to his servants then 'No-one can hold back his hand or say to him: "What have you done?" ' (4:35). Indeed an essential part of God's power is that he does know 'the end from the beginning, from ancient times, what is still to come' (Isa. 46:10). I have argued especially in the commentary on Chapter 11 that this in no way reduces humans to puppets because the multiplicity of human choices and events make genuine decisions possible at every stage.

At root the question is one of revelation. Has God spoken and has he made himself and his unfolding purposes known? The stance taken in this commentary is that the book is a genuine sixth century product which not only unfolds the inner meaning of the Exile but prepares believers for the time of the End, foreshadowed in the régime of Antiochus Epiphanes but relevant for all who live in the 'Last Days'. This theme is developed further in the commentary proper.

3. What kind of a book is it?
Daniel is usually described as an example of Apocalyptic literature but that is far too narrow a definition, and as the

commentary shows many different kinds of genre are employed.

There is first of all a strong story line in the book; not just in the sense of the series of stories in Chapters 1–6 but in the unfolding narrative sequences in Chapters 7–12. This reminds us that Daniel is an important part of the Bible's plot-line, the story from Creation to Consummation. The term often used for this is 'meta-narrative', i.e. the story of God's purposes into which individual narratives must be fitted. Moreover, the story-telling in the book shows considerable skill in plot, character-isation, setting and literary techniques. I have particularly explored this in the commentary on Chapter 3, the story of the Blazing Furnace, perhaps the most exciting episode in the book.

There are also strong links with Wisdom Literature. Daniel and his friends are the wise (see e.g. 1:17 and 12:3). They live their lives according to the fear of the Lord (see Proverbs) and, like Job and Ecclesiastes, the book is much concerned with the providence of God and the meaning of life.

Nevertheless Daniel does have many Apocalyptic features both in style and substance. Apocalyptic characteristically employs visions, dreams, symbols, heavenly messengers and a preoccupation with the End. The battle between light and darkness is sharp, and earthly events are shown to be echoes of greater cosmic events. It should not be too sharply distinguished from prophecy, not least because of the Apocalyptic sections in other books (e.g. Isaiah 24–27 and Zechariah 1–8).

The Exile raised acutely the nature of God's kingdom and divine intervention in history. However, it did not exhaust the meaning of these, and taking particularly the time of Antiochus, the author shows how history is working to an end which will not be achieved by political evolution or revolution but by divine intervention.

It is in Christ that all the many hopes and visions of Daniel are to be fulfilled. By his coming 'for us and for our salvation' he suffers like Daniel and his friends, but by dying he also makes possible the eternal life anticipated in 12:2. By his coming again he will finally establish the kingdom that will never be destroyed and thus cause the wise to *'shine like the brightness of the heavens'* (12:3).

Apocalyptic is a wide term, and concerns both the 'now' and 'not yet' of the kingdom. Both are important in Daniel because while God's people must live in Babylon their strength to live there comes from their citizenship in the heavenly Jerusalem.

4. The Structure of the Book

Readers will gain most from the book of Daniel if they read it as a whole and get a sense of its flow and direction. Chapter 7 is the hinge of the book, providing both a basis for the stories and an overview for the visions. Chapters 8–12 deal in more detail with certain parts of the picture but the scope of Chapter 7 is the whole of human history.

Chapter 1 corresponds to Chapter 12 in its portrait of Daniel the wise man, and his continuing anticipating the eternal glory of the wise in the latter chapter.

Chapters 2 and 7 give an overview of human power in history and both of these are followed by chapters which give us selected glimpses of that power and how it relates to God's power (in story in 3–6 and in vision in 8–12:3).

The whole book bears the hallmarks of careful planning and selection which underlines its main theme: God will be God and the world will know it.

1

Dare to be a Daniel

For a book which is to take the reader into the most mysterious and spectacular events, Daniel opens in a very low key manner. Yet we do not have to look far below the surface to find the great issues and themes which are to dominate the book. Indeed a proper understanding of Chapter 1 is essential to give us our bearings in the often puzzling material which follows.

The structure of the chapter is threefold. Verses 1 and 2 place the story in the context of world history; verses 3-20, the main bulk of the chapter, tells how Daniel and his friends come to prominence and face their first big test; verse 21 is a historical note which points to the end of the Exile and shows that Daniel was significant in that entire period.

The Historical Setting (1:1-2):

[1]In the third year of the reign of Jehoiakim king of Judah, Nebuchadnezzar king of Babylon came to Jerusalem and besieged it. [2]And the LORD delivered Jehoiakim king of Judah into his hand, along with some of the articles from the temple of God. These he carried off to the temple of his god in Babylonia and put in the treasure-house of his god.

It is impossible to underestimate the devastating effect of the Exile in Babylon to the Jewish people. Their God appeared to be weaker than the gods of Babylon, their holy city was destroyed, and their temple burned and its vessels removed.[1] The story here, however, is brief and unemotional. Certainly this is not the final devastating sack of the city (for which see 2

---

[1] See Introduction pp. 11-13 for a fuller discussion of the Exile and its impact on Jewish life and thinking.

Kings 24:10–25:21), but the first raid on the city in 605 BC which was to be followed by a further capture of the city in 597 and the final destruction in 587. However, from the perspective of the author all this had already happened and the whole question of whether God was in control was an agonisingly real one.

Three factors, of great significance for the book, emerge in these first two verses. The first is the placing of the story among the realities of contemporary power politics. Nebuchadnezzar, the vigorous young king of the new Babylonian empire, which had risen on the ruins of the fallen Assyrian empire, was the most powerful figure on the scene. Against him the feckless figure of Jehoiakim, the puppet king of the tiny state of Judah, was no opposition at all.[2] The paralleling of the names of Babylon and Jerusalem symbolise not simply two states, but the conflict between the city of the world and the city of God in every generation. This story, therefore, is not merely a piece of ancient history, it is a word to every generation of the faithful, and part of the purpose of the commentary is to apply the text as well as expound it.

This is particularly underlined by the second emphasis in these verses. The rise to power of Nebuchadnezzar was not ultimately due either to his superior military strategy or to the weakness of his opponents; it was a deliberate action by the Lord of history. 'The LORD delivered[3] Jehoiakim king of Judah into his hand.' Significantly God is called 'LORD'; the Exile is not a devastating setback to his plans; he remains in control and will use the events to work out his purpose.

Thirdly, the specific reference to 'the articles from the temple of God' is significant. This is one of the many hints of the

---

[2] Difficulties have been raised over the dating of Daniel 1:1. For a helpful discussion of these see D. J. Wiseman: *Nebuchadnezzar and Babylon*, O.U.P. 1987, – esp. pp. 23ff. where he points out that the phrase translated in the NIV as 'besieged it' can mean simply 'showed hostility to' and that the resulting activity could simply have been a result of his threatening behaviour.
[3] The word the NIV translates 'delivered' is 'nathan' – the normal Hebrew verb 'to give'. This is very important in the theology of the book where all power is a gift from God – see e.g. 2:37; 4:25; 5:18; 7:6; 8:12.

profounder meaning of the Exile. Like the Exodus this was a conflict between the God of Israel and pagan gods, with this time Yahweh appearing to have been defeated.[4] These vessels are to feature later in the drunken orgy of Belshazzar in Chapter 5; and, given the sense of horror with which Babylon[5] was regarded, the action would appear particularly impious.

So in a few brief phrases, the main issues and concerns of the book are outlined. This is to be about power and who is in control. It is to be about appearances and reality, about the way God works out his purposes.

Dare to be a Daniel (1:3-20):

With the vital historical and theological background in place, the author now focuses on how it all affects four young men. The Exile happened to real people, and if its implications for faith and life are not simply to remain high-sounding theories, these have to be worked out in actual lives. Thus the author begins the characteristic feature of Chapters 1–6 which is a number of stories about Daniel and his companions.[6]

This first story is soberly and concisely told, with none of the visions and cosmic drama which occur later, and yet it is vital in establishing the tone and atmosphere of the whole book. What this story emphasizes and indeed embodies is a particular life-style; how to live for God and be faithful to him in an unsympathetic environment. Chapter 11:32 speaks of 'the people who know their God', and Chapter 1 is vital in demonstrating what that means. As we shall see, the thrust of this chapter is to drama-tise the choices that God's people in every age must make as

---

[4] Perhaps the key text for understanding the biblical interpretations of the Exodus is Exodus 12:12: *'I will pass through Egypt ... and I will bring judgment on all the gods of Egypt. I am the LORD.'*

[5] It is a pity that the NIV has not kept the archaic term 'Shinar' in verse 2 which links Nebuchadnezzar's action with that early arrogant monarch 'Nimrod, the mighty hunter' (Genesis 10:8-11) and with the location of that monument to human pride – the tower of Babel. The name also occurs in Zechariah 5:11 as a centre of evil.

[6] See Introduction p. 18 for a discussion of the structure of the book.

they try to live a godly life in the midst of an alien culture.

First, the author introduces us to the situation and the main personalities:

> ³Then the king ordered Ashpenaz, chief of his court officials, to bring in some of the Israelites from the royal family and the nobility – ⁴young men without any physical defect, handsome, showing aptitude for every kind of learning, well informed, quick to understand, and qualified to serve in the king's palace. He was to teach them the language and literature of the Babylonians. ⁵The king assigned them a daily amount of food and wine from the king's table. They were to be trained for three years, and after that, they were to enter the king's service.
>
> ⁶Among these were some from Judah: Daniel, Hananiah, Mishael and Azariah. ⁷The chief official gave them new names: to Daniel, the name Belteshazzar; to Hananiah, Shadrach; to Mishael, Meschach; and to Azariah, Abednego.

Presumably removing these kind of people would both weaken Judah and bring new blood into Babylon. These were people who already had the advantages of birth and education. The language used of them closely resembles that employed of Joseph who was 'a discerning and wise man' (Gen. 41:33) and reminds the reader of an earlier man of God who rose to prominence in a foreign court. Terms such as 'wise', 'understanding', 'insight', forms of which occur here in verse 4, recall the Wisdom tradition of books such as Proverbs. All this points to something else: in Ancient Israel, Wisdom is inextricably bound up with 'the fear of the Lord' and inevitably the reader wonders what will happen when the wisdom comes into contact with Babylonian wisdom which is likewise bound up with the worship of Babylonian gods.

This issue arises straight away with the mention of the two areas most significant in the story: **the language and literature of the Babylonians** (v. 4) and **food and wine from the king's table** (v. 5). What is interesting is to see Daniel's response to these two issues; he, and his friends, participate fully in the training programme but made a stand over the issue of eating, and that second issue is dealt with in some detail in the later verses.

Exactly what they would be studying is clear from the phrase **language and literature of the Chaldeans**.[7] In Daniel, 'Chaldeans' refers particularly to the sages or soothsayers who were an important group in advising the king. Much of their study would involve magic, sorcery, divination and astrology (see e.g. 2:2). When about to embark on an expedition or to determine policy the king would consult with them, and we shall see in Chapter 2 how a disturbing dream is regarded as their concern.

The practical relevance of this is that we need to be familiar with the cultural and intellectual attitudes of our world. This will mean study and familiarity with many attitudes and view points which are alien to the gospel. It is not only possible but necessary if we are to be effective witnesses in our culture. The *practice* of divination and sorcery was forbidden to the Jews (Deut. 18:10-12; 1 Sam. 28:3ff.), but the understanding of it and interacting with it was a very different matter. To be effective for God in Babylon involved a serious attempt to understand Babylon.

The three year training period has proved to be a remarkably durable length of time for such activity. Like Moses they were to be thoroughly immersed in the culture and lifestyle of one of the world's great empires. Another sign of Nebuchadnezzar's determination to integrate these young men fully into Babylonian society was their being given new names with elements of the names of Babylonian gods. This again was a common practice: Joseph was named Zaphenath-Paneah and Esther was also known as Hadassah. Once again Daniel makes no protest; what is important is that his heart does not belong to Babylon.

Outwardly, then, the king had cause for satisfaction. His programme was under way and his favoured candidates had accepted with apparent willingness the drastic change in their lifestyle and status. For these young people (and Daniel and his friends were only a few – see verse 6: **Among these ...**) the splendid and awesome city of Babylon must have made

---

[7] The NIV again, rather unhelpfully, renders this as 'Babylonians'.

Jerusalem seem an insignificant backwater. With its gorgeous palaces lining the mighty Euphrates, its magnificent Hanging Gardens, its military conquests and its unimaginable wealth it must have both fascinated and intimidated. Yet it is not on any of the obvious issues that Daniel decides to make a stand and the story now takes an unexpected turn.

> [8]But Daniel resolved not to defile himself with the royal food and wine, and he asked the chief official for permission not to defile himself in this way. [9]Now God had caused the official to show favour and sympathy to Daniel, [10]but the official told Daniel, 'I am afraid of my lord the king, who has assigned your food and drink. Why should he see you looking worse than the other young men of your age? The king would then have my head because of you.'

The first thing to notice is the word **resolved** – literally 'placed in his heart'. This was a definite and settled decision arrived at by Daniel and in no sense a gesture. Commentators[8] differ in their explanations of why it was this issue of food and drink. It does seem to be a minor point and yet it is clearly the crux of the chapter and essential to our understanding of the book.

It has been argued that the palace rations would probably have been 'offered to idols' (see 1 Cor. 8), but that is not mentioned as an issue in other parallel stories – e.g. Joseph, Moses and Esther, and the same would apply to vegetables. Similarly attempts to argue that eating meat would break the food laws of the Torah do not wholly explain the issue. It is true that Leviticus 3:17 prohibits the eating of fat and blood as does Leviticus 17:10-14, and presumably these regulations and also the ban on pork were not observed at the Babylonian court. This does not, however, explain the refusal of wine. Most certainly the passage is not advocating vegetarianism and teetotalism. People may for particular reasons adopt these as right for them but they are not givens of the gospel – 'the kingdom of God is not a matter of eating and drinking' (Rom. 14:17). Moreover

---

[8] See the useful discussion in Goldingay, pp. 18-19.

this was clearly not a permanent prohibition as is clear in 10:3: 'I ate no choice food, no meat or wine touched my lips ... until the three weeks were over.' There again, for a particular reason and for a specific time, Daniel is practising this kind of self-denial, and the implication is that he would normally eat meat and drink wine.

Perhaps the true explanation lies somewhere else. For every believer there comes a moment of decision, an issue where a stand must be made and the choice will determine the whole future character of life. For Daniel that issue was food from the king's table. Studying Babylonian science and culture and bearing Babylonian names could be undertaken with loyalty to God unimpaired. Eating with all its implications of fellowship and solidarity could not. Indeed the very fact that the passage is difficult to interpret is in itself significant. What we have here is not a blueprint with detailed instructions about how to act in any given situation. Rather the concern is with basic attitudes and discipleship. For Daniel it was food, for others it may be vast wealth (like the rich young ruler in the Gospels), for others ambition or relationships. The key issue is that for all of us there is a point at which we must choose to go on in the way of faithfulness to God or to compromise.

Verse 9 shows how God not only overrules the great issues of the rise and fall of empires but is intimately concerned with everyday matters. This shows Daniel's courage; there was no guarantee that the official would act in this sympathetic way. In any case we move now to the plan Daniel suggests.

[11]Daniel then said to the guard whom the chief official had appointed over Daniel, Hananiah, Mishael and Azariah, [12]'Please test your servants for ten days: Give us nothing but vegetables to eat and water to drink. [13]Then compare our appearance with that of the young men who eat the royal food, and treat your servants in accordance with what you see'. [14]So he agreed to this and tested them for ten days.

Having made a stand on the matter of principle, Daniel is prepared to be flexible on details. He does not expect the officials to share his convictions nor does he want a public display of his beliefs. He is content that God knows his heart, and he is gracious and pragmatic in providing a way for the official both to be loyal to the king and sympathetic to his charges.

> [15]At the end of the ten days they looked healthier and better nourished than any of the young men who ate the royal food. [16]So the guard took away their choice food and the wine they were to drink and gave them vegetables instead.
>
> [17]To these four young men God gave knowledge and understanding of all kinds of literature and learning. And Daniel could understand visions and dreams of all kinds.

Two matters are now prominent; the first is the result of the experiment with the food and the second is the general link of this with God's overall purpose.

As to the first. It would be to trivialise the story to say that it proves that vegetarian food is better for your health; although as I write these words the news media is full of warnings of 'mad cow disease'. What is more important is that God honours faithfulness to his word. This does not mean (see especially Chapters 3 and 5) that all dangers magically disappear. Rather it is God's way of establishing firmly the young men in this pagan environment and of encouraging them to further faithfulness.

Secondly, verse 17 links this incident with the whole sequence of events. The important word 'gave' occurs again and reminds us that everything is under God's control. This underlines God's approval of the action the young men took in relation to the literature and learning of Babylonia. It is an interesting reminder that while they worked hard and, as already emphasised (v. 4), were highly intelligent, the ability to succeed in their studies was a gift of God. This conviction prevented in them, and will similarly in us, a prideful intellectualism. It is also a powerful reminder that opportunity to study is to be received as an opportunity to serve God and treated as a sacred trust from him.

I think a further point is being made: since all knowledge and wisdom are from God, the good insights and useful knowledge from all cultures are part of his generous gift to human beings. As such these are not to be despised but recognised as part of the wisdom God dispenses.

The second part of the verse makes this point in a different way. Daniel was given the special gift of understanding visions and dreams. This is important in a number of ways. Babylonian wisdom depended on sorcery and divination and a mark of a wise man was to be able to interpret dreams (see Chapter 2). For Daniel to have credibility in that situation he needed to be able to demonstrate not only equal but superior ability to the Chaldeans. Moreover, he needed God-given wisdom to discern the true meaning of those dreams. His knowledge of God and his will would mean that there was no danger of imagining that his own intellect or some magical process was behind his success (see 2:27-30). The rest of the book is to demonstrate how genuine was Daniel's gift and how faithfully he used it. This leads to the conclusion of the story which forms the main bulk of this chapter.

> [18]At the end of the time set by the king to bring them in, the chief official presented them to Nebuchadnezzar. [19]The king talked with them, and he found none equal to Daniel, Hananiah, Mishael and Azariah; so they entered the king's service. [20]In every matter of wisdom and understanding about which the king questioned them, he found them ten times better than all the magicians and enchanters in his whole kingdom.

These verses contain hints of much that is to come in subsequent chapters. Superior attainments seldom lead to popularity particularly when displayed by outsiders, and the vindictiveness of the establishment in Chapters 3 and 5 is an example of this. **Ten times better** need not be taken literally; it is a standard way of saying immeasurably superior. The phrase **they entered the king's service** (v. 19) literally is 'they stood before the king'. It would have been better to have kept this phrase

with its echo of the description of a prophet of God. Thus in 1
Kings 17:1 Elijah speaks of 'Yahweh, God of Israel before whom
I stand' (see, e.g. New King James Version). Since Daniel and
his friends have stood in the court of heaven they are not going
to be overawed by the court of Babylon. The chapter, which
begins with the humiliation of Judah and its royal house, ends
with some of that house in a leadership role in Babylon. This
had not happened by force or intrigue but by the overruling hand
of God. But before we leave the chapter there is one further
stage to go.

The Future Perspective (1:21):

And Daniel remained there until the first year of King Cyrus.

If the year of Daniel's exile was 605, the date referred to here is
539. Probably a boy in his late teens in Chapter 1, he would be
well advanced in his eighties when the Babylonian empire fell
to Cyrus the Persian. Just as verses 1 and 2 established important
principles for understanding the book, so this verse gives us a
long perspective. Jeremiah 25:12 predicted a seventy year exile,
and this is vital for the theology of God's control of history. As
we shall see, particularly in Chapters 7–12, while human power
can be awesome it is always given a specific time; only one
kingdom lasts for ever.

The rise and fall of the Babylonian empire was not due to
some abstract pattern of history which with iron logic decreed
that events would follow a particular pattern. Rather events are
in the hand of the God of Israel who is also God of the nations
and God of heaven and who 'gives' and withholds power. It is
interesting to see how this positive note is paralleled at the end
of the historical section of the book:

So Daniel prospered during the reign of Darius and the reign of
Cyrus the Persian (6:28).

Whatever the circumstances, whoever the human agent in power,

God will protect his people. Even more strikingly at the end of the Apocalyptic section of the book, beyond the trials and difficulties of this present life there is a hope and inheritance which is lasting:

> 'As for you, go your way till the end. You will rest, and then at the end of the days you will rise to receive your allotted inheritance' (12:13).

The name 'Cyrus' symbolises the end of Exile. Isaiah indeed speaks of Cyrus as God's 'shepherd' and 'anointed' (Isa. 44:28 and 45:1), and in these chapters the prophet is speaking not only of the end of Exile, but of the End and the coming of God's kingdom.

General Comments:
As we have seen, Chapter 1 is an essential foundation for understanding the whole book and it would be useful at this point to mention basic assumptions which will both round off our study of the chapter and introduce the next stage.

The first basic assumption is that God is in control; formidable powers stand against him, huge obstacles are in his path, but his purposes cannot be thwarted. This is no abstract doctrine. This is worked out in the harsh world of power politics. Moreover it extends to the details of personal living and to such basic matters as eating, drinking, learning and working. Knowing a God like that is the only way to stand firm among the treacherous cross currents of an alien culture and indeed to outlast that culture.

The second assumption is that revelation and insight are needed to discern what God's will is in these confusing circumstances. These are not primarily gained by study and intelligent application but by openness to God and an acknowledgement of his gifts. Vision and revelation are at the heart of the book of Daniel because simply looking at world events without a key to interpret them will lead to despair rather than hope. That key is the nature of God revealed in his living word. We have already seen how this chapter draws on other Scriptures and we shall see this even more clearly as we continue our study. If we want to hear what God is saying and see what God is doing we must know Scripture.

The third basic assumption complements this. To be effective for God we also need to know our own context and discover where the points of crisis will come. We need to listen to the news and current affairs programmes, read newspapers, be familiar with politics, society, culture, music, arts and as much as we can of contemporary culture. Only then will we be able to be effective communicators in our society and speak the eternal truths of the gospel in ways which will relate to contemporary people and their concerns.

Fourthly, this chapter is fundamentally about the kind of attitudes and lifestyle appropriate for those living in an alien environment. As we saw in our analysis of verses 8-10 the issue of food was a specific one for Daniel and his friends in that context. For each of us there will be issues specific to our context where we will need to make a stand. That stand will determine the course of our lives and our future usefulness to God.

Questions for further study:

1. What is 'Babylon' in your world?

2. What issues would lead you to 'resolve' (v. 8) that the time has come to make a stand?

3. Why should Babylonian culture apparently be acceptable and Babylonian food not?

2

What dreams may come

Dreams hold a never-failing fascination. Any large bookshop has a section devoted to dreams, visions, premonitions and second sight. Behind this fascination lurks a sense of vulnerability and insecurity and a desire to have at least some control over the future by knowing what it will be. This is now the situation in which Nebuchadnezzar finds himself early in his reign. The next three chapters place him centre stage, giving a fascinating glimpse into his personality as well as carrying on the theology and history of the book. This long chapter, which we shall divide into seven sections for ease of comment, not only gives us Nebuchadnezzar's dream and its interpretation, but provides background which is essential to understanding these.

The situation (2:1-14)

> [1]In the second year of his reign, Nebuchadnezzar had dreams; his mind was troubled and he could not sleep. [2]So the king summoned the magicians, enchanters, sorcerers and astrologers to tell him what he had dreamed. When they came in and stood before the king, [3]he said to them, 'I have had a dream that troubles me and I want to know what it means.'
>
> [4]Then the astrologers answered the king in Aramaic, 'O king, live for ever! Tell your servants the dream, and we will interpret it.'
>
> [5]The king replied to the astrologers, 'This is what I have firmly decided. If you do not tell me what my dream was and interpret it, I will have you cut into pieces and your houses turned into piles of rubble. [6]But if you tell me the dream and explain it, you will receive from me gifts and rewards and great honour. So tell me the dream and interpret it for me.'

⁷Once more they replied, 'Let the king tell his servants the dream, and we will interpret it.'

⁸Then the king answered, 'I am certain that you are trying to gain time, because you realise that this is what I have firmly decided: ⁹If you do not tell me the dream, there is just one penalty for you. You have conspired to tell me misleading and wicked things, hoping the situation will change. So then, tell me the dream, and I will know that you can interpret it for me.'

¹⁰The astrologers answered the king, 'There is not a man on earth who can do what the king asks! No king, however great and mighty, has ever asked such a thing of any magician or enchanter or astrologer. ¹¹What the king asks is too difficult. No-one can reveal it to the king except the gods, and they do not live among men.'

¹²This made the king so angry and furious that he ordered the execution of all the wise men of Babylon. ¹³So the decree was issued to put the wise men to death, and men were sent to look for Daniel and his friends to put them to death.

¹⁴When Arioch, the commander of the king's guard, had gone out to put to death the wise men of Babylon, Daniel spoke to him with wisdom and tact.

Power is what this chapter is about and Nebuchadnezzar finds himself threatened by a realm he cannot control and is both frightened and frustrated. In a manner, which we are soon to learn is characteristic, he summons the whole galaxy of **magicians, enchanters, sorcerers and astrologers**; a summons which reveals his desire to appear in charge and is to demonstrate how woefully inept the whole establishment is.[1] Indeed one of the major points of this section of Daniel is to show how ineffective the establishment is and how in a multitude of ways it has to be rescued by the outsider.

The demand of the king (v. 3) shows us an early indication of what is to be a major feature of chapters 2–4 which is his

---

[1] 'Magicians' is also used of Egyptian enchanters (Gen. 41:8; Exod. 7:11); 'enchanters' is unique in Daniel, but in Syriac means 'snake charmer'; 'sorcerers' would use incantations and omens; as already noted in Chapter 1 'astrologers' are in fact 'Chaldeans'.

excessive expectations. The reply of the **astrologers** (v. 3) reveals the emptiness of their pretensions. The author is fond of using irony and this is evident here, **O king, live for ever** is a hollow joke; the dream, which they do not know, shows that clearly.[2]

However, the atmosphere turns distinctly unpleasant in verses 5ff. and the king threatens the astrologers with violent death if they fail to answer his question. Nebuchadnezzar's anger is fearsome and we might think unwarranted. Yet the author is exposing the emptiness of the occult establishment. If they had real knowledge it would be no more difficult to recount than to interpret the dream. As had been said in 1:17 and is about to be demonstrated God has given Daniel that ability. As the confrontation continues in verses 8-11 the irony of the situation is explored further. The king is almost certainly right in alleging that they **were trying to gain time**. However, his further accusation that they are conspiring against him probably reflects his insecurity rather than the reality. There is a further irony in verse 11: **No-one can reveal it to the king except the gods**[3] **and they do not live among men**. It is not long before Nebuchadnezzar is to encounter a God who is anything but remote and who is to appear right before his terrified eyes. In any case the king's anger brings events to a dangerous climax and a decree is issued to kill the wise men including Daniel and his friends.[4]

This introduction has been no mere space-filler. It has cleverly built up a picture of a volatile and insecure Nebuchadnezzar ready to use his power in an arbitrary way. It has likewise exposed the hollowness of the 'wise men' of Babylon. But it has done more. The echoes of Genesis 41 and Exodus 7 are powerful reminders that the God of the Patriarchs and the God of the

---

[2] The Aramaic part of the book begins here in verse 4 and continues to the end of Chapter 7. It is interesting that it is used in both parts of the book. See Introduction p. 15 for further discussion.

[3] It is possible that 'the gods' may have a singular meaning here.

[4] The mention of 'Daniel and his friends' heightens the dramatic tension of the story. It is a narrator's comment and does not imply that they either were or were not present at the original meeting.

Exodus is at work behind the scenes and we are not surprised when Daniel comes into greater prominence.

Daniel's Intervention (2:14-19a)

14When Arioch, the commander of the king's guard, had gone out to put to death the wise men of Babylon, Daniel spoke to him with wisdom and tact. 15He asked the king's officer, 'Why did the king issue such a harsh decree?' Arioch then explained the matter to Daniel. 16At this, Daniel went in to the king and asked for time, so that he might interpret the dream for him.

After the frenetic atmosphere of the last few verses it is evident that Daniel's calm is a deliberate contrast. Notice also his tact; he questions the sudden and hasty nature of the order and thus gains time from the king who was probably by then regretting his precipitate command. The matter now moves on to a higher plane and a very different perspective is introduced.

17Then Daniel returned to his house and explained the matter to his friends Hananiah, Mishael and Azariah. 18He urged them to plead for mercy from the God of heaven concerning this mystery, so that he and his friends might not be executed with the rest of the wise men of Babylon. 19During the night the mystery was revealed to Daniel in a vision.

How Daniel uses the time is important. He spends it in prayer and involves his friends. Prayer is to be vital in Daniel's life (see e.g. Chs. 5, 9 and 10) and this is a reminder of how prayer alone can reach that world from which revelation comes. Not by horoscopes, seances and divination would enlightenment come, but from the **God of heaven**, a title also used in the post-Exilic books of Ezra and Nehemiah. This is not simply the tribal God of Israel but the God who rules the heavenly bodies, the study of and attempt to manipulate which lay at the heart of Babylonian religion.

Thus the solution is **revealed** to Daniel. He did not work it out or imagine it. What is revealed is the **mystery** – a word used

only here and in 4:9. The word also occurs in the Dead Sea
Scrolls as a technical term for a riddle which needs God's
explanation, a meaning very close to that in the New Testament.
The technicalities of how Daniel received the vision are not given
either here or elsewhere (see e.g. 7:1); the important detail is the
'fact' of the revelation not its 'method'.

Daniel's Psalm (2:19b-23)

The greater reality behind the visible reality of court politics is
now crystallised in a vivid and memorable song of praise. The
Old Testament frequently includes such poems: notably the Song
of the Sea (Exod. 15); the Song of Deborah (Judg. 5); the Song
of Hannah (1 Sam. 2:1-10); and the prayers or psalms of Jonah
(Ch. 2) and Habakkuk (Ch. 3). In the New Testament we have
the Magnificat (Luke 1:46-55), and the frequent passages where
Paul becomes lyrical (e.g. Phil. 2:5-11; 1 Tim. 3:16), as well as
the many times when the book of Revelation breaks into song
(e.g. 4:11; 5:9-10; 13-14; 15:3-4) and 19:1-2, 5, 7-8). This has
the effect of making the truths embodied in song more than
dogma, they are worship. This psalm of Daniel is a song which
can be appreciated both as a timeless ascription of praise and
also as intimately related to the specific circumstances.

Then Daniel praised the God of heaven ²⁰and said:
    Praise be to the name of God for ever and ever; wisdom and
power are his.'

The psalm begins with the grounds of Daniel's confidence. The
name of God for a Jew is Yahweh, the Lord of the covenant
who is committed to his people by promises that he cannot and
will not break. **Wisdom** is that profound knowledge and understanding which comes only from revelation. **Power** is no
abstraction but revealed in God's activity in history.

²¹'He changes times and seasons; he sets up kings and deposes
them. He gives wisdom to the wise and knowledge to the
discerning.

²²He reveals deep and hidden things, he knows what lies in darkness, and light dwells with him.'

That power and wisdom is now more clearly specified and a theology of history is outlined which prepares us for the dream which embodies and illustrates that theology. In Babylon, an empire that seemed established and permanent, Daniel declares his faith in a God for whom it is merely an episode. It is a development of the idea that sovereignty is 'given' which we saw in Chapter 1. But this way of looking at history is itself a gift of God: **He gives wisdom to the wise**. The fundamental knowledge of God is because he is light and nothing is obscure or hidden to him. Daniel now applies this specifically to his own situation:

²³'I thank and praise you, O God of my fathers: You have given me wisdom and power, you have made known to me what we asked of you, you have made known to us the dream of the king.'

These words express Daniel's own sense of the immense privilege of being allowed to share in God's perspective and be part of his purpose. A number of observations can be made at this point. We are halfway through this long chapter and have not yet reached the dream or its interpretation. Part of this is the writer's technique; he knows the value of suspense in building up and holding interest. If the book were being serialised, undoubtedly this would be a cliff-hanger, and we would eagerly await the next episode to find out what was going to happen.

But there is a deeper point. The theology of this psalm remains true whether we are given a specific revelation of God's purpose in particular events or not. Goldingay puts this well:

Most of the time, however, the people of God have to live without revelations of this kind, yet they are still called to affirm that power and wisdom with Daniel on the basis of a revelation in prospect but yet unseen.[5]

---

[5] Goldingay. p. 57.

Indeed as we shall see in later chapters there is much that Daniel does not know (e.g. 7:27; 12:9) and thus faith remains essential.

Daniel and Nebuchadnezzar (2:24-30)

In a few deft strokes, the writer takes us to the actual dream in a meeting of Daniel and Nebuchadnezzar.

> 24Then Daniel went to Arioch, whom the king had appointed to execute the wise men of Babylon, and said to him, 'Do not execute the wise men of Babylon. Take me to the king and I will interpret his dream for him.'
>
> 25Arioch took Daniel to the king at once and said, 'I have found a man among the exiles from Judah who can tell the king what his dream means.'
>
> 26The king asked Daniel (also called Belteshazzar), 'Are you able to tell me what I saw in my dream and interpret it?'
>
> 27Daniel replied, 'No wise man, enchanter, magician or diviner can explain to the king the mystery he has asked about, 28but there is a God in heaven who reveals mysteries. He has shown King Nebuchadnezzar what will happen in days to come. Your dream and the visions that passed through your mind as you lay on your bed are these:
>
> 29'As you were lying there, O king, your mind turned to things to come, and the revealer of mysteries showed you what is going to happen. 30As for me, this mystery has been revealed to me, not because I have greater wisdom than other living men, but so that you, O king, may know the interpretation and that you may understand what went through your mind.'

Daniel shows the tact we have now come to expect from him (v. 24). Problems have been raised about verses 25-26 which appear to suggest that Nebuchadnezzar had not previously met Daniel and that it was Arioch who had taken the initiative. However, it is plain that Arioch would want to claim maximum credit for himself. As far as Nebuchadnezzar's failure to acknowledge earlier acquaintance is concerned, Montgomery makes the shrewd comment: 'royal minds are easily forgetful of "college

professors".'[6] The name 'Belteshazzar' (v. 26) links this with
the earlier story in 1:6-7.

The right context for both the dream and its interpretation is
established in verses 27 and 28. Daniel repudiates any idea that
he is a more skilful 'astrologer' and gives glory to God. We
may compare Joseph's words to Pharaoh in Genesis 41:16: ' "I
cannot do it," Joseph replied to Pharaoh, "but God will give
Pharaoh the answer he desires." ' Once again the NIV has rather
obscured part of the text; in verse 28 it reads **what will happen
in days to come**. More literally the text reads 'what will be in
the latter days'. This could simply mean 'in the future', i.e. 'in
the days to come'; but the inescapable emphasis that the Kingdom of God with its goal of the End has broken in is missed.

Daniel relates this to the king's own musings about the future
(v. 29) as he lay awake. The fact that dreams frequently reflect
their preoccupations is simply another way of saying that God
works through normal means and does not diminish the value
of the revelation. The astrologers *et al* were right to say (v. 11)
that only divine revelation could solve the riddle but wrong in
assuming that this would not happen.

The Dream (31-35)
Now we are ready to hear the details of the dream which is of an
enormous dazzling statue.

> [31]'You looked, O king, and there before you stood a large statue –
> an enormous, dazzling statue, awesome in appearance.'

That the king should dream of such a statue is not particularly
surprising; we know that statues of Marduk occupied prominent places in Babylon and other cities. Baldwin further points
out that it was not uncommon for kings and others to lie at the
feet of an image of a god in a temple to ask for guidance.[7]

---

[6] Montgomery, p. 161.
[7] Baldwin, p. 97.

[32]'The head of the statue was made of pure gold, its chest and arms of silver, its belly and thighs of bronze, [33]its legs of iron, its feet partly of iron and partly of baked clay.'

The four metals symbolise the variety of the natural resources of the earth. As in Chapter 7, four suggests universal scope as in 'the four corners of the earth' or, the four rivers of Eden (Gen. 2:10-14). Gold and silver stand for wealth, and bronze and iron for power. However, the admixture of clay, an incompatible element, suggests a fatal weakness. It is this weakness which proves its undoing.

[34]'While you were watching, a rock was cut out, but not by human hands. It struck the statute on its feet of iron and clay and smashed them. [35]Then the iron, the clay, the bronze, the silver and the gold were broken to pieces at the same time and became like chaff on a threshing-floor in the summer. The wind swept them away without leaving a trace, But the rock that struck the statue became a huge mountain and filled the whole earth.'

The insubstantial nature of the statue is vividly evoked by its dissolving into chaff. We must not press this literally and unimaginatively; it is a dream where images melt into each other. The rock, however, grows until it covers the earth. We may recall Habakkuk 2:14: 'The earth will be filled with the knowledge of the glory of the LORD as the waters cover the sea.'

The Interpretation (36:45)
It is important to realise that the dream itself is not revelation, rather it is raw material for revelation. That this is so can be shown first by looking at Chapter 7 where the substance of that revelation is further developed as it arises from a very different vision. The explanation is needed, because without this, all kinds of interpretations would be possible. Both picture and word are needed; they belong together and appeal to both heart and mind.

[36]'This was the dream, and now we will interpret it to the king. You, O king, are the king of kings. The God of heaven has given you dominion and power and might and glory; [37]in your hands he has placed mankind and the beasts of the field and the birds of the air. [38]Wherever they live, he has made you ruler over them all. You are that head of gold.'

Daniel here shows a fine blend of respect for Nebuchadnezzar, using his titles, but at the same time an uncompromising loyalty to God. The rule over not only earth and humans but animal life as well echoes Genesis 1:28. Many problems arise about the identification of these four kingdoms, and these will be looked at in the exposition of Chapter 7. That will be a more appropriate place because here the interpretation emphasises the first and last kingdoms and only mentions the others. Undoubtedly Nebuchadnezzar would be flattered at hearing the words, **You are that head of gold**. Moreover, the rest of the interpretation with its implication that the destruction of the statue would be long after his time would set his immediate fears to rest.

[39]'After you, another kingdom will rise, inferior to yours. Next, a third kingdom, one of bronze, will rule over the whole earth.'

More is to be said on this period, especially in Chapters 7ff. but what is being emphasised is that God 'changes times and seasons'. The author, however, has more to say about the fourth kingdom:

[40]'Finally there will be a fourth kingdom, strong as iron – for iron breaks and smashes everything – and as iron breaks things to pieces, so it will crush and break all the others.'

This seems, at first sight, to contradict verse 44 where it is the kingdom of heaven which as a rock shatters all four kingdoms. However, the theology of history of Daniel can accommodate this under God's overruling providence which uses human activity to work out his purpose.

Moreover this kingdom is vulnerable to its own internal contradictions:

41'Just as you saw that the feet and the toes were partly of baked clay and partly of iron, so this will be a divided kingdom; yet it will have some of the strength of iron in it, even as you saw iron mixed with clay. 42As the toes were partly iron and partly clay, so this kingdom will be partly strong and partly brittle. 43And just as you saw the iron mixed with baked clay, so the people will be a mixture and will not remain united, any more than iron mixes with clay.'

Iron suggests an authoritarian régime which carries out repressive policies and tries to coerce the 'clay'. Verse 43 perhaps refers to a policy of intermarriage ('so the people will be a mixture'), a policy unwelcome to the Jews. The fundamental weakness of this régime is evident and, as in the dream, the interpretation turns to the intervention from the outside.

44'In the time of those kings, the God of heaven will set up a kingdom that will never be destroyed, nor will it be left to another people. It will crush all those kingdoms and bring them to an end, but it will itself endure for ever. 45This is the meaning of the vision of the rock cut out of a mountain, but not by human hands – a rock that broke the iron, the bronze, the clay, the silver and the gold to pieces.

'The great God has shown the king what will take place in the future. The dream is true and the interpretation is trustworthy.'

It is not clear who **these kings** (v. 44) are; presumably the rulers of the fourth kingdom. This new sovereignty will be different in kind from any other, not least in its permanence. While God has hitherto worked in human history, that history is to be brought to an end. The process by which this will happen and the nature of that sovereignty is not specified here; we learn more of that in Chapter 7 but fuller revelation must await the coming of the King himself. Yet partial glimpses of that rule are given from time to time and the believer has to live in the time between the times when the kingdom has already come in Christ, and yet its ultimate fulfilment lies in the future. Meanwhile we must trust the word which is here described as **trustworthy**.

The Aftermath (46-49)
Nebuchadnezzar is as intemperate in his gratitude as he had earlier been in his threats (v. 5):

> 46"Then King Nebuchadnezzar fell prostrate before Daniel and paid him honour and ordered that an offering and incense be presented to him.'

He did not concern himself further with the message of the dream. For the moment, at least, he was secure and reverted to the role of gracious sovereign bestowing gifts.

> 47The king said to Daniel, 'Surely your God is the God of gods and the Lord of kings and a revealer of mysteries, for you were able to reveal this mystery.'

This is something less than an acknowledgment that Daniel's God is the only true God (for that we must wait until Chapter 4). He remains a polytheist and can accommodate another god, admittedly a rather powerful one – **God of gods and Lord of kings**. He focuses on God as **revealer of mysteries**, rather than the one who 'changes times and seasons' (v. 21)

The chapter ends with a return to the political scene and promotion for Daniel and his friends.

> 48Then the king placed Daniel in a high position and lavished many gifts on him. He made him ruler over the entire province of Babylon and placed him in charge of all its wise men. 49Moreover, at Daniel's request the king appointed Shadrach, Meschach and Abednego administrators over the province of Babylon, while Daniel himself remained at the royal court.

Life must go on even after the stunning revelations of this chapter and this is indicated in verses 48 and 49. Daniel's position as head of the wise men is an extension both of the opportunities and difficulties of Chapter 1, and we may be certain that this blend of unyielding loyalty on principle and ability to be flexible in secondary issues would serve him well now as then. Similarly his loyalty to his friends is shown by including them in his new and improved circumstances. This also explains how they are at the centre of the drama in Chapter 3 while Daniel is absent. Daniel is literally 'at the gate of the king'. The gate was the centre of administration in the ancient Near East and the phrase suggests Daniel was a member of the cabinet. The three friends became provincial governors outside the city itself.

General Comments

Three issues raised by the chapter require a little further consideration. The first is the relationship this chapter illustrates between the eternal and the contemporary. The truths about God revealed are timeless: indeed that is the essence of the truth about him, that he is unlimited by time. His sovereignty and his providence are truths about God in every generation. But they remain at the level of 'blessed thoughts' unless they are lived out in the reality of present experience. As we have seen, these issues were very literally life and death for Daniel and his friends and had profound consequences for their own personal futures. Similarly the reader of Daniel needs to look at the contemporary world with those same convictions, although there is little evidence that God reigns. At the time of writing continuing trouble in Iraq, the faltering progress of the Ulster peace talks and renewed tension between Israelis and Palestinians re-emphasize the need for faith. Earlier generations feared nuclear holocaust, world communism and, earlier still, Viking raids and the instability after the fall of the Roman Empire. The point is that each generation has to learn this lesson again. Similar applications can (and particularly in Chapter 1 have been) be made to personal lives. Belief in the rule of God is essential for the life of faith.

This is linked with the second issue which is the place of revelation. We cannot simply read events because, as already mentioned, most of the time they will suggest that God is not reigning. That is why the writer shows us that we have to look beyond the events to their interpretation. This does not mean that we can, Daniel-like, make instant identifications between prophetic passages and world events. There has been, and still is, a kind of writing which has seen books such as Daniel as providing detailed blueprints of contemporary events.[8] Thus the fourth kingdom is variously the EEC, world communism (Russian or Chinese), and 'the little horn' of the parallel vision in Chapter 7 is Hitler, Stalin or Saddam Hussein. If these and similar interpretations are taken as illustrations of general principles that is one thing, but to regard any of these as the only legitimate interpretation is futile and self-defeating.

The chapter also throws light on the method of revelation which is a blend of picture and word. There is a half-truth that 'a picture is worth a thousand words'. But even when contemplating a picture our thoughts and sensations are being verbalised. Here the picture on its own would have been incomprehensible or misleading. If Daniel had simply outlined the dream without the interpretation, what would have been more natural than for Nebuchadnezzar to have assumed that he was the rock which broke the image to pieces? Without the words of explanation the dream would have remained a fascinating but impenetrable vision.

Yet the words without the picture would have been theoretical and difficult to apply. The description of the image has both a haunting eeriness and solidity which wonderfully conveys both the elusiveness and solidity of the power. Similarly its rapid pulverising shows the insubstantial nature of power. Our imaginations as well as our minds are gripped. So it is that, like Daniel, we are moved to praise God.

It is revelation which helps us to live in the contemporary in the light of the eternal and gives to us our third issue which is the chapter's theology of history. Only a brief comment is nec-

---

[8] See, for example, Hal Lindsey: *The Late, Great Planet Earth* (Grand Rapids, Zondervan, 1970).

essary here because we shall discuss it more fully in the exposition of Chapter 7. The conviction expressed here is that God is the Lord of history who works out his purpose in the apparently meaningless flux of events. It is this conviction which underlies the Hebrew Bible's description of Joshua to Kings as the 'Former Prophets'; history whether past, present or future is no mystery to God. How this bears on the question of predictive prophecy and how God's sovereignty relates to human freedom we shall discuss in Chapter 7.

Questions for further study

1. Are dreams still a legitimate way of discovering God's will?

2. Can we use this chapter to predict the future?

3. What do we mean when we pray, 'Your kingdom come' ?

3

With God in the flames

With Chapter 3 the whole question of where real power lies is no longer simply a matter of international politics and the dreams and ambitions of the powerful; it comes to focus on how in a situation of extreme danger personal loyalty will face the supreme test. Shadrach, Meshach and Abednego had successfully handled the popularity test in Chapter 1 and now they fear the sinister power of a police state. This raises, in a dramatic form, the question of which king and which kingdom, because it is above all a story of power: power to influence people, to control events, to get what we want.

Once again, and even more strikingly, a well-told story is being used to make points about God, miracle and human behaviour. We shall look at how the techniques of the story teller transport us into the ancient oriental world, catch us up in the flow of events and enable us to see how this story speaks to our story. I want to suggest that the chapter is a drama in three acts, each of which dramatises an aspect of power.

The Apparent Power of Nebuchadnezzar (3:1-12)
The opening verses set the scene and dramatise the issues:

> ¹King Nebuchadnezzar made an image of gold, ninety feet high and nine feet wide, and set it up on the plain of Dura in the province of Babylon.

Just as Nebuchadnezzar had dreamed of power embodied as a fearsome statue he now goes one better and has one built, representing probably a god or perhaps even himself. In any case it was a deliberate linking of political and religious allegiance, and thus a challenge to every aspect of the faith and lifestyle of the three young Jews. The proportions of the statue ('ninety feet high and nine feet wide') are extraordinary and intended to impress and intimidate. This briefly sketched setting is followed by a roll call of the pomp and circumstances of Babylon which serves to show the unequal nature of the contest: the whole machinery of the state against three young men.

[2]He then summoned the satraps, prefects, governors, advisers, treasurers, judges, magistrates and all the other provincial officials to come to the dedication of the image he had set up. [3]So the satraps, prefects, governors, advisers, treasurers, judges, magistrates and all the other provincial officials assembled for the dedication of the image that King Nebuchadnezzar had set up, and they stood before it.

[4]Then the herald loudly proclaimed, 'This is what you are commanded to do, O peoples, nations and men of every language. [5]As soon as you hear the sound of the horn, flute, zither, lyre, harp, pipes and all kinds of music, you must fall down and worship the image of gold that King Nebuchadnezzar has set up. [6]Whoever does not fall down and worship will immediately be thrown into a blazing furnace.'

[7]Therefore, as soon as they heard the sound of the horn, flute, zither, lyre, harp and all kinds of music, all the peoples, nations and men of every language fell down and worshipped the image of gold that King Nebuchadnezzar had set up.

The impressive and overwhelming nature of the scene is emphasised by a repeated roll-call of names representing the power of Nebuchadnezzar.[1] This is reinforced by the fanfare of wind

---

[1] The list of officials is probably in rank order. 'Satraps' were rulers over the main provinces of the Persian Empire and 'prefects' were probably their deputies. Governors were in charge of the sub-divisions of the satrapies. (Nehemiah was a governor). The other officials were in charge of various functions of government. Some have argued that since the vocabulary reflects the Persian period this is one of the indications that the book is late. This need not be the case; it could simply be that later editions of the book have updated some of the terms. This is a common enough practice: e.g. a modern historian writing about Roman Eboracum would naturally call it York.

and stringed instruments.[2] If this is not enough to bully into submission, the threat of a horrible death for failure to comply with the order is introduced: **Whoever does not fall down and worship will be thrown into a blazing furnace** (v. 6).

The writer has shown enormous skill in building up atmosphere. The repetition of the awesome names are like nails hammered into the young men's coffins. The sense of the overwhelming numbers and solidarity of the Emperor's entourage highlights their isolation. The blaring music sounded like their death knell and the whole world had turned bleak and hostile. It is always a real test of faith and courage to stand for truth in a climate of hostile public opinion. In our world of mass media and the global village the pressure of opinion is probably more subtle but no less intense.

The way the story is told invites two observations. The first is the reason why I have called this section the 'apparent' power of Nebuchadnezzar. There is irony at work here as the writer subtly ridicules human power. There is something rather ridiculous at the thought of all the good and the great falling on their faces before a lifeless statue at the sound of a musical medley. We can almost hear the mocking words of Isaiah 40:19:

> As for an idol, a craftsman casts it, and a goldsmith overlays it with gold and fashions silver chains for it.

There is surely satire too in the repetition of the lists, as if mere mouthing of titles created the reality of authority. How effectively too, he catches their attitude of servility. Verse 7 reads, **As soon as they heard ... they fell down**. More literally, the text could be translated: 'As they were hearing ... they were falling down.' The impression is of these great officials and others almost tripping over each other in their eagerness to demonstrate total loyalty. Behind all human power and glory there is a note of transience. As Shakespeare wonderfully puts it:

---

[2] The musical instruments in some cases have Greek names but this could either be explained as names borrowed from trading links, or as with the officials, names updated by later editors.

> The cloud-capped towers,
> The gorgeous palaces, the solemn temples,
> The great globe itself, yea all who it inhabit,
> Shall like this insubstantial pageant faded,
> Leave not a rack behind.[3]

But for all its hollowness, there is also a sinister and evil side to this power. The Babylonian state is demanding total loyalty. This is a reply in more frightening circumstances of the demands made on them in Chapter 1. Nebuchadnezzar is supported by all the power and privilege of his great empire and will stand no opposition.

The story is told of two British diplomats of the Victorian era who were granted an audience with the Shah of Persia. At the entrance to his throne room they were curtly instructed by an official to crawl into the Shah's presence. Drawing themselves up to their full height they replied that they were certainly not going to give to any foreign ruler a courtesy which their own most gracious Sovereign Lady did not demand. The prestige of Queen Victoria and, perhaps even more, the fear of British gunboats saved them from any punishment. But here, the three young men had no powerful supporters and no allies on whom to call.

This story, characteristically for Old Testament narrative, does not explicitly state what was in either Nebuchadnezzar's or the young men's minds. We deduce the arrogance of the one and the faith of the others from the way the story is told, the techniques we have already noticed. But with verse 8 the story moves up a gear and the first act ends with a cliff-hanger:

> [8]At this time some astrologers came forward and denounced the Jews. [9]They said to King Nebuchadnezzar, 'O king, live for ever. [10]You have issued a decree, O king, that everyone who hears the sound of the horn, flute, zither, lyre, harp, pipes and all kinds of music, must fall down and worship the image of gold, [11]and that whoever does not fall down and worship will be thrown into a

---

[3] William Shakespeare: The Tempest. Act IV.

blazing furnace. [12]But there are some Jews whom you have set over the affairs of the province of Babylon – Shadrach, Meshach and Abednego – who pay no attention to you, O king. They neither serve your gods nor worship the image of gold you have set up.

As the drama of the first act continues, once again we have to listen carefully to what the story is saying. We are not told why the 'astrologers' (v. 8) acted as they did, but there are some hints in the text. The first is the repeated use of the word 'Jews' (verses 8 and 12). Their motive is partly at least racial; they are jealous that people in this conquered nation have been promoted. In verse 12 they come as near as they dare to criticising Nebuchadnezzar – **whom you have set over the affairs of the province of Babylon.** We see a similar motive at work in Haman in 'Esther'. The second is the use of the term **astrologers** (v. 8) or 'Chaldeans'. They may still have been resentful at Daniel's ability to interpret Nebuchadnezzar's dream in Chapter 2. So to ethnic prejudice is added professional as well as political jealousy.

However, a further hint in the text takes us to a deeper level and shows us the real issue at stake. The NIV translation 'denounced' in verse 8 is rather weak. The Aramaic expression is a vivid one: literally 'tear and eat the flesh', and some such word as 'slander' would be more appropriate. In the Syriac language the noun from the phrase is used of the devil. The devil is the 'accuser of our brothers, who accuses them before our God day and night' (Rev. 12:10). Here is the underlying thrust of this story: the accuser is not Babylonian but devilish. This is the kingdom of darkness attempting to destroy the children of light. In fact this is the theme of the whole book dramatised in this story.

All of this has been horribly witnessed again in our own century. As I write these words in 1995 the fiftieth anniversary of the end of World War II, the events of the Holocaust have again been burned on the world's consciousness. Goldingay quotes from an article in *The Times* of 29th July 1936 which illustrate the godlike pretensions of the state which led to the Holocaust. In that article, Herr Baldur von Schirach declared: 'Whoever serves Adolf Hitler, the Führer, serves Germany, and whoever serves Germany serves God.'[4] When the state claims godlike powers it becomes a ravenous monster which soon creates its martyrs of those who will not bow to its pretentions. The repetition of the fanfare of musical instruments and the second mention of the threat of the fiery furnace increase suspense and bring us to the end of this first movement of the chapter.

The Apparent Weakness of God (13-23)

We have already seen how the Exile itself appeared to demonstrate to the world that the God of the Exodus had lost his power. The second act is introduced by the confrontation of Nebuchadnezzar with the dauntless three:

> [13]Furious with rage, Nebuchadnezzar summoned Shadrach, Meshach and Abednego. So these men were brought before the king, [14]and Nebuchadnezzar said to them, 'Is it true, Shadrach, Meshach and Abednego, that you do not serve my gods or worship the image of gold I have set up? [15]Now when you hear the sound of the horn, flute, zither, lyre, harp, pipes and all kinds of music, if you are ready to fall down, and worship the image I made, very good. But if you do not worship it, you will be thrown immediately into a blazing furnace. Then what god will be able to rescue you from my hand?'

Another element now adds even greater tension to the story: the rage of Nebuchadnezzar. In many respects, as we have seen, Nebuchadnezzar was a fairly tolerant and enlightened king. Yet where his own prestige is involved he has already shown himself to be prone to furious outbursts of anger. In 2:12: 'This made the king so angry and furious that he ordered the execution of all the wise men of Babylon.' This heightens our fear for the young men in their dreadful predicament. Suspense is further

---

4 Goldingay, p. 73.

increased by the king's interrogation and the repetition of the by-now sinister sounds of music, and the fiery furnace is no longer a general threat but specific for the three.

Yet once again the writer hints at deeper issues and gives a hint of the eventual outcome: **Then what god will be able to rescue you from my hand?** (v. 15). 'Hand' is often a metaphor for power in the Old Testament. In Chapter 1:2 the author says of Nebuchadnezzar: 'And the LORD delivered Jehoiakim, King of Judah into his hand.' Nebuchadnezzar here thinks that he is controlling events. He has clearly forgotten the words of Daniel: 'The God of heaven has given you dominion and power and might and glory; in your hands he has placed mankind and the beasts of the field and the birds of the air' (2:37-38). Failure to realise that his own hand is powerless leads to this impasse, and is to cause further trouble in Chapter 4.

> [16]Shadrach, Meshach and Abednego replied to the king, 'O Nebuchadnezzar, we do not need to defend ourselves in this matter. [17]If we are thrown into the blazing furnace, the God we serve is able to save us from it, and he will rescue us from your hand, O king. [18]But even if he does not, we want you to know, O king, that we will not serve your gods or worship the image of gold you have set up.'

Now for the first time in the story the three young men speak. What they say is one of the finest expressions of the daring faith which is the hallmark of this book. **We do not need to defend ourselves** is not rudeness but an appeal to Nebuchadnezzar to realise the unreasonableness of the course of action he is pursuing.

Then they confront the fiery prospect head on. There are translation problems in verses 17 and 18 but the general sense is plain enough. They appeal to a realm where Nebuchadnezzar's writ does not run. God's ways are mysterious and even if they perish in the flames they will believe in their God and his love. Indeed this is what many believers have found. No supernatural hand has shielded them from agonising death. When Latimer and Ridley were burned for their faith in Oxford no last minute intervention saved them. Yet the victory of faith overcame the world. 'Play the man, Ridley,' said Latimer, 'and by God's grace we will light this day in England a candle that will never be put out.' The moment of confrontation has come.

> [19]Then Nebuchadnezzar was furious with Shadrach, Meshach and Abednego, and his attitude towards them changed. He ordered the furnace to be heated seven times hotter than usual [20]and commanded some of the strongest soldiers in his army to tie up Shadrach, Meshach and Abednego and throw them into the blazing furnace. [21]So these men, wearing their robes, trousers, turbans and other clothes, were bound and thrown into the blazing furnace. [22]The king's command was so urgent and the furnace so hot that the flames of the fire killed the soldiers who took up Shadrach, Meshach and Abednego, [23]and these three men, firmly tied, fell into the blazing furnace.

Events now move swiftly and the three are seized and bound by some of the toughest soldiers. Baldwin[5] suggests that the furnace may have been tunnel shaped and bricked up at one end, and that would certainly provide a feasible interpretation of the scene which is now played out. The utter hopelessness of the men and the impossibility of rescue is emphasised by the circumstantial detail. The mention of their clothes (v. 21) builds up further suspense and the unexpected deaths of the executioners underlines the certainty of their fate.

Thus this second movement of the chapter shows God's cause collapsing in apparently irretrievable disaster. Just as the Exile had swallowed up their nation, so this holocaust is set to consume these young men. So much of history has bleakly appeared to confirm the helplessness of God. The Victorian hymn writer Faber expresses this powerfully:

> He hides himself so wondrously,
> As if there were no God.
> He is least seen when all the powers
> of ill are most abroad.

---

5. Baldwin, p. 103.

The Real Power of God (24-30)

By every logical criterion the story ought to end here. The absolute power of Nebuchadnezzar over life and death has been vindicated. God has not intervened and the men's destruction seems inevitable. Yet it is just at this point that there is an amazing turn of events and these form Act 3.

24Then King Nebuchadnezzar leaped to his feet in amazement and asked his advisers, 'Weren't there three men that we tied up and threw into the fire?'

They replied, 'Certainly, O King.'

25He said, 'Look! I see four men walking around in the fire, unbound and unharmed, and the fourth looks like a son of the gods.'

26Nebuchadnezzar then approached the opening of the blazing furnace and shouted, "Shadrach, Meshach and Abednego, servants of the Most High God, come out! Come here!'

It certainly seems to be all over. The king gazes idly into the flames and begins to imagine he is seeing things. Firelight does indeed play strange tricks, and those who remember the days of coal fires will recall how easy it was to imagine pictures forming among the flames. For a moment or two he must have thought he was seeing things or even that he had dozed off in the heat and was dreaming. His fury giving way to blind panic he leaps up and stammers out: **Weren't there three men ... we threw into the fire?** Surely Nebuchadnezzar, king of Babylon, king of the world, could count up to three!

Then came the moment of truth. With terrible suddenness the awful truth dawned. This was no dream. This was no nightmare. It was far worse than any nightmare. Their God had taken up the gauntlet and without blaring music, entourage or the trappings of authority had appeared in the flames beside his people. Nebuchadnezzar and all his glory had been simply marginalised.

Quickly recovering himself, Nebuchadnezzar covers his confusion by calling the men to come out of the furnace. By giving commands he feels more in control of the situation. But his world will never be the same again.

I have so far concentrated on the skill of the narrator and tried to bring out something of the power of the story. What we must examine now is the actual miracle. I think we do not properly understand it if we try to rationalise it along the lines that fakirs and others have survived fire and other extreme conditions in a state of trance. There is not a scrap of evidence for this in the story. Nor on the other hand should we simply generalise it into a statement that God will be with his people in their troubles. Something much bigger is happening.

When we remember that the main concern of the book of Daniel is with who has ultimate power we begin to see more clearly what this story is saying. The life of the world to come, the kingdom of God of which Daniel had spoken in Chapter 2, had broken into this world. Just as Jesus walked on water and raised the dead, so that world to come had here invaded this one. How this miracle happened is not explained, but that is the invariable biblical pattern. The fact is stated and the activity of God is emphasised. The real power of God is shown by his complete bypassing and disregard of the power of Nebuchadnezzar, although the king will not fully realise this until Chapter 4:35: 'He does as he pleases with the powers of heaven and the peoples of the earth. No-one can hold back his hand or say to him: "What have you done?" '

I shall say a little more on the place of miracle in my general remarks at the end of the commentary on Chapter Three but something needs to be said on the last phrase in verse 25: **and the fourth looks like a son of the gods.** The Authorised Version translated this as 'the Son of God' and saw in it a pre-incarnation appearance of Christ. Many modern commentators prefer some such translation as 'angel' which would suggest a representative of God. I think two things can be said.

The first is that for Nebuchadnezzar the fourth figure is certainly a divine being. He was a deeply religious man, superstitious even. The eerie dream of Chapter 2 would have made him particularly sensitive to the supernatural world. As far as he was concerned, a god, and a more powerful one than any he had yet encountered, was active.

The second is that the God of the Old Testament is regularly presented as intervening in his creation. From the walking in the Garden of Eden, the mysterious visitor at Abraham's tent, the enigmatic figure Joshua meets outside the walls of Jericho, as well as here and elsewhere in Daniel, the 'angel of the Lord' in effect brings God's own presence right into the affairs of the world. The whole question of angels will be discussed especially in Chapters 4 and 10, but it is important to note here that they appear throughout the Bible as God's agents. But whatever exactly the 'angel of the Lord' means it is plain that it is part of the whole preparation for a God who one day is to become one of us. It is true that God suffers in the flames with his children, and when they do not escape from the furnace he will be there with them. This is the conviction of Isaiah: 'When you walk through the fire, you will not be burned; the flames will not set you ablaze' (Isa. 43:2).

Ultimately this story is part of that great story where God takes our humanity, and unjustly tried and condemned is put to death and yet destroys death and rises again. This is eloquently put by Russell:

'In the leaping flames of the furnace we see the shape of a cross and beyond that a garden with an empty tomb.'[6]

The other noteworthy point here is that Nebuchadnezzar now refers to the God of Israel as **the most High God**. Surely here is a name which cuts every Nebuchadnezzar down to size and since it is Nebuchadnezzar himself who uses that name, he is now effectively acknowledging the real power of God. Names such as *Most High* and the *God of Heaven*, while they occur earlier, become particularly prominent during and after the Exile, as Israel begins to look outwards and emphasise a God of universal

6. Russell, *Active Volcano*, p. 48.

and not only Jewish significance. This emphasizes the message of Chapter 2 that 'He changes times and seasons; he sets up kings and deposes them' (2:21).

²⁶So Shadrach, Meshach and Abednego came out of the fire, ²⁷and the satraps, prefects, governors and royal advisers crowded around them. They saw that the fire had not harmed their bodies, nor was a hair of their heads singed; their robes were not scorched, and there was no smell of fire on them.

²⁸Then Nebuchadnezzar said, 'Praise be to the God of Shadrach, Meshach and Abednego, who has sent his angel and rescued his servants! They trusted in him and defied the king's command and were willing to give up their lives rather than serve or worship any god except their own God. ²⁹Therefore I decree that the people of any nation or language who say anything against the God of Shadrach, Meshach and Abednego be cut into pieces and their houses be turned into piles of rubble, for no other God can save in this way.'

³⁰Then the king promoted Shadrach, Meshach and Abednego in the province of Babylon.

After the high drama of the previous verses, the third act of the story returns to the more prosaic world of politics. The fearsome roll call of the good and the great at the beginning of the chapter has now become a gaggle of curious onlookers who cannot quite believe their own eyes. Nebuchadnezzar, now back in control of the world he knows best, promotes the three and decrees universal respect for their God. We should not read too much into this. Nebuchadnezzar is making Judaism a recognised religion and forbidding anyone to discriminate against it. He is still far from personal faith, and only the experiences of Chapter 4 will lead to that. There is a fine irony here. The apparent weakness of these men and their God led to greater power than would have been the case if they had not been faithful. To quote Faber again:

Thrice-blest is he to whom is given,
The instinct that can tell,

That God is on the field, when he,
Is most invisible.

Nebuchadnezzar has still to learn the deeper significance both
of his dream and the events of this chapter, but before we leave
Chapter 3 I would like to make some general comments which
will help to crystallise some of the main issues.

General Comments

By any standards, Daniel 3 is a brilliant story, probably the most
exciting story in the book. That is why it is important to do
justice to its narrative qualities and not simply read it to find
'lessons'. If we are committed to the authority of Scripture, that
includes taking seriously the literary form in which books are
written. The world of the story catches our imagination and
engages our sympathy. The plight of the three young men, alone
in a hostile world, is vividly conveyed and reminds us that this
is often the lot of those who stand for truth.

That is why the techniques already mentioned are so important
in a true assessment of the chapter. The lists of officials repeated
sonorously show the overwhelming weight of state power. Yet
it also creates a rather mocking and satirical atmosphere.
Similarly the fanfare of instruments is deliberately underlined,
reminding us of the sinister as well as the inspiring power of
music. The ominous refrain 'thrown into a blazing furnace' builds
up heart-stopping suspense. We can also note the effective use
of dialogue and indeed the whole sweep of the chapter. All this
makes an imaginative response to it essential if we are to do
justice to its depths.

Out of the story grows the theology. This is no set of
abstractions, this is a real and dangerous world in which our
belief that the Lord reigns is going to be tested to the utmost
limits. It is never easy to escape being over-impressed by human
greatness and influence, and a robust faith in the reality of the
other world is needed. This does not mean 'other-worldliness'.
No book deals more with the unseen world than Daniel and yet

all the main characters are busily involved in the world of politics. As we saw in Chapter 1, Daniel and his friends belong to both worlds, but their conduct in this contemporary situation is governed by their link with the eternal world.

The relationship of faith and miracle is also well brought out in the story. The magnificent declaration of verse 18 – **But even if he does not, we want you to know, O king, that we will not serve your gods or worship the image of gold you have set up** – leads to swift and relentless punishment. There is no guarantee or even probability that they will be saved. That is why this miracle must be understood properly. The world to come broke into this one in a spectacular way. But the life of the world to come belongs to the world to come and this story gives no support to an unbalanced triumphalism. God will be in the furnace with his people and will rescue them. But that rescue may involve the resurrection to eternal life which lies beyond death. This miracle, in other words, is a 'token' one, a window thrown open into the ultimate triumph of God rather than a blueprint for most of our earthly experiences.

After Chapter 3 we hear no more about Shadrach, Meshach and Abednego. This again is not insignificant. The stories and visions of the book are concerned with the reign of God and the precise significance of the human involvement in that is known to God alone. They take their place among the nameless heroes of Hebrews 11:32ff., one of whose acts of faith is described as 'quenched the fury of the flames' (v. 34).

This chapter's power then arises from a combination of well-told story and powerful theology. It is a call to robust and daring faith even in the circumstances where there is no guarantee that God will intervene. Yet in spite of its excitement and narrative flow there is no sensationalism or over-elaboration. The choice is stark and the response unambiguous.

Questions for further study

1. Why does God not always save his people from the flames?

2. What is the point of this story?

3. What do we learn about God from this incident?

4

Judgment and mercy

This chapter is one of the most striking in the book and contains a most amazing statement of biblical theology from Nebuchadnezzar himself. Once again, as in Chapter 2, there is a dream and an interpretation but the whole atmosphere is very different, and its impact on the king far more profound. This is the fourth and last glimpse of the life of Nebuchadnezzar; he very much embodied the Babylonian empire, and our final picture of that empire is to be its downfall in Chapter 5. It is presented as a kind of open letter from Nebuchadnezzar. Verses 19-33, the account of the interpretation of the dream and the king's madness, are written in the third person for dramatic reasons as we shall see. Once again the chapter is carefully constructed and shows a fine dramatic and theological sense.

The King's testimony (4:1-3)[1]
Nebuchadnezzar begins his statement in a characteristic way with his name and those whom he is addressing:

> King Nebuchadnezzar,
> To the peoples, nations and men of every language who live in all the world:
> May you prosper greatly.

The reminder of the power of Nebuchadnezzar and his right to be heard by a world-wide constituency makes what follows staggering. He acknowledges that there is a sovereignty greater than his and a kingdom unlimited by time:

---

[1] In the Aramaic text these verses stand as 31-33 of Chapter 3. It is important to remember that our chapter divisions are not inspired.

²'It is my pleasure to tell you about the miraculous signs and wonders that the Most High God has performed for me.

³How great are his signs,
    how mighty his wonders!
His kingdom is an eternal kingdom;
    his dominion endures from generation to generation.'

Doubt has been expressed about Nebuchadnezzar using language like this which is reminiscent of the Psalter. Two points can be made. Daniel's influence on the king's thinking and language cannot be discounted. Secondly, Baldwin makes the point that in the Babylonian creation epic the god Marduk is conceived in very similar terms.[2] Most striking of all, as Goldingay points out,[3] is that Nebuchadnezzar in this age and at the height of his power is giving to God the honour promised for the end of the Age and thus briefly anticipating the kingdom.

Fears and Doubts (4:4-9)
Yet all is not well and, as on that much earlier occasion in Chapter 2, fear of the unknown returns to haunt the king.

⁴'I, Nebuchadnezzar, was at home in my palace, contented and prosperous. ⁵I had a dream that made me afraid. As I was lying in my bed, the images and visions that passed through my mind terrified me.'

Two small details place in focus what follows. The first, not in the Aramaic text, but in the Old Greek story of Daniel,[4] is that this episode happened in the eighteenth year of Nebuchadnezzar's reign. In Jeremiah 52:29 this is given as the year of the final fall of Jerusalem and the exile of the whole nation. The king's contentment would no doubt be partly at least satisfaction at the end, as he saw it, of this tiny but troublesome nation.

---

[2] Baldwin, p. 110.
[3] Goldingay, p. 91.
[4] A whole cycle of Daniel stories exists; some in Aramaic and some in Greek. Probably the best known is the Prayer of the Three Young Men in the Fur-

He could not have realised, even in his openness to God, how that nation was to survive his own and be destined still to play a crucial role in the coming of the eternal kingdom.

The second is the word translated **prosperous** in verse 4. This word has connotations of luxury and can mean, for example, the thick foliage of a tree. This prepares the alert reader for the dream of the tree and hints at the pride of the king. He has indeed acknowledged God but has still much to learn. Again fears and scruples shake him: not, as in Chapter 2, the insecurities of the earlier part of his reign, but the fear of the supernatural and the trembling he had already experienced in Chapter 3 as the terrifying God of Israel had marginalised and confounded him.

Again we have a parade of the wise men, Daniel arriving last:

> 6"So I commanded that all the wise men of Babylon be brought before me to interpret the dream for me. 7When the magicians, enchanters, astrologers and diviners came, I told them the dream, but they could not interpret it for me. 8Finally, Daniel came into my presence and I told him the dream. (He is called Belteshazzar, after the name of my god, and the spirit of the holy gods is in him). 9I said, "Belteshazzar, chief of the magicians, I know that the spirit of the holy gods is in you, and no mystery is too difficult for you. Here is my dream; interpret it for me."'

There is nothing here of the fury of the king and the hasty commands to execute the wise men as in Chapter 2. Perhaps this reflects the king's increased maturity or his confidence in Daniel. It is important to notice that Nebuchadnezzar does not worship Daniel's God because he specifically names him 'Belteshazzar' calling attention to the fact that this name was given 'after the name of my god'. He does indeed recognise the supernatural nature of Daniel's wisdom but this should not be overplayed as both the queen (5:11) and Belshazzar (5:14) use the same expression. Nevertheless we must not ignore the deeper

nace which appears in the Morning Office of the Anglican Book of Common Prayer, known as the 'Benedicite'.

point the author is making. The meaning of history cannot simply
be read from events. Insight from God is needed and we shall
discuss this further in Chapter 7.

The Dream (4:10-18)
This dream takes the form of a sacred tree, a symbol common to
religious traditions, for example, Ygdrasil, in Norse myth which
joined heaven and earth. Goldingay helpfully points out that
this is a symbol of security:

> Humanity finds ways of reassuring itself that the life and resources
> of the cosmos are secure. The myth of all-providing science has
> recently offered that reassurance in our history; the myth of the
> cosmic tree offered it to the Ancient Near Eastern World.[5]

Ezekiel speaks of the Pharaoh in 31:6 as a cedar of Lebanon,
and earlier in that chapter of Assyria as another cedar: 'All the
birds of the air nested in its boughs, all the beasts of the field
gave birth under its branches; all the great nations lived under
its shade.' So we are dealing with a common symbol.

> [10]'These are the visions I saw while lying in my bed: I looked, and
> there before me stood a tree in the middle of the land. Its height
> was enormous. [11]The tree grew large and strong and its top touched
> the sky; it was visible to the ends of the earth. [12]Its leaves were
> beautiful, its fruit abundant, and on it was food for all. Under it the
> beasts of the field found shelter, and the birds of the air lived in its
> branches; from it every creature was fed.'

The tree represents Nebuchadnezzar at the zenith of his power,
and its beauty as well as its strength is emphasized. In his power,
however, he feels strong enough to be gracious, and the benevo-
lent effects of his rule are emphasized. So far, so good; but there
is another part to the dream.

---

[5] Goldingay, p. 92.

¹³'In the visions I saw while lying in my bed, I looked, and there before me was a messenger, a holy one, coming down from heaven. ¹⁴He called in a loud voice: "Cut down the tree and trim off its branches, strip off its leaves and scatter its fruit. Let the animals flee from under it and the birds from its branches. ¹⁵But let the stump and its roots, bound with iron and bronze remain in the ground, in the grass of the field.

"Let him be drenched with the dew of heaven, and let him live with the animals among the plants of the earth. ¹⁶Let his mind be changed from that of a man and let him be given the mind of an animal till seven times pass by for him.

"¹⁷The decision is announced by the messengers, the holy ones declare the verdict, so that the living may know that the Most High is sovereign over the kingdoms of men and gives them to anyone he wishes and sets over them the lowliest of men."

¹⁸'This is the dream that I, King Nebuchadnezzar, had. Now, Belteshazzar, tell me what it means, for none of the wise men in my kingdom can interpret it for me. But you can, because the spirit of the holy gods is in you.'

This next stage of the dream is introduced by a **watcher**[6] who is also a **holy one**, who in contrast to the tree growing from earth comes down from heaven. This is related to the common Old Testament picture of the heavenly court or council. Some examples are Psalm 82 where God stands in the council of the gods to give judgment; Job 1 and 2 where Satan presents himself at that court; and 1 Kings 22:8ff. where Micaiah speaks of it: 'I saw the LORD sitting on his throne with all the host of heaven standing round him on his right and left.' The idea was particularly common in Babylon and is echoed in Ezekiel's vision (Ezek. 1:17-18). It also occurs in Zechariah 4:10: '... the eyes of the LORD which range throughout the earth.' It is related to the idea of God 'seeing', not just in the sense of a casual glance, but of close supervision and guidance. It is interesting in that connection to study the use of the word 'see' in the creation

_____

[6] NIV 'messenger' is probably not right; it appears to be reading the text as *syr* (envoy) rather than *'yr* (watchman); although the Greek text simply has 'angelos'.

account of Genesis 1. Yahweh, says Psalm 121:4, 'neither slumbers nor sleeps'; he is awake and active while humans dream. The 'watcher, the holy one' is an example of what is put in the language of doxology in Psalm 103:20-21:

> Praise the LORD, you his angels,
>   you mighty ones who do his bidding,
>   who obey his word.
> Praise the LORD, all his heavenly hosts,
>   you his servants who do his will.

The watcher commands the tree to be cut down; it is not specified who is to do this, presumably other heavenly beings. The imagery then changes from a tree to an animal and indeed that animal is to become a human deprived of his senses. This sequence is quite common in a dream where images blend into each other and it prepares us for the interpretation. Now the power represented by this great tree is to be reduced to a pitiable shadow of itself and while once it sheltered others now it cannot even shelter itself from being drenched with dew and roosting among the animals.

The fact that **the decision is announced by the messengers, the holy ones** (v. 17) does not contradict that it is **the decree the Most High has issued**. They are the agents and executors; they do not initiate, they carry out. The **seven times** occurs here first, although 'times' is common in the later part of Daniel and is generally taken to mean a year. The fact that the **Most High is sovereign over the kingdoms of men** is visible to the eye of faith, but the point of the dream is to make this plain to others especially to Nebuchadnezzar himself. Unlike the dream of Chapter 2 the meaning of the dream seems less of a problem. However, the failure of the king and his wise men to understand it introduces an element of suspense and leads into the interpretation.

The Interpretation (4:19-27)

Daniel does not proceed to an interpretation immediately:

> [19]Then Daniel (also called Belteshazzar) was greatly perplexed for a time, and his thoughts terrified him. So the king said, 'Belteshazzar, do not let the dream or its meaning alarm you.'

It is unlikely that Daniel feared for his own life nor for the general interpretation of the dream but rather for the new element, i.e. the king's madness.

> Belteshazzar answered, 'My lord, if only the dream applied to your enemies and its meaning to your adversaries!'

Here Daniel shows his characteristic courtesy and genuine concern for Nebuchadnezzar. The interpretation which follows is likewise restrained and as favourable as possible:

> [20]'The tree you saw, which grew large and strong, with its top touching the sky, visible to the whole earth, [21]with beautiful leaves and abundant fruit, providing food for all, giving shelter to the beasts of the field, and having nesting places in its branches for the birds of the air – [22]you, O king, are that tree! You have become great and strong; your greatness has grown until it reaches the sky, and your dominion extends to distant parts of the earth.'

The description here makes no reference to the king's pride and could be read as a celebration of the positive and beautiful aspects of Babylonian civilisation. Yet there are hints of the arrogance which inspired the building of the tower of Babel reaching to the heavens (Gen. 11:4).

> [23]'You, O king, saw a messenger, a holy one, coming down from heaven and saying, "Cut down the tree and destroy it, but leave the stump, bound with iron and bronze, in the grass of the field, while its roots remain in the ground. Let him be drenched with the dew of heaven; let him live like the wild animals, until seven times pass by for him." '

The repetition of the details gives an ominous sense of impending doom.

> [24]'This is the interpretation, O king, and this is the decree the Most High has issued against my lord the king: [25]You will be driven away from people and will live with the wild animals; you will eat grass like cattle and be drenched with the dew of heaven. Seven times will pass by for you until you acknowledge that the Most High is sovereign over the kingdoms of men and gives them to anyone he wishes. [26]The command to leave the stump of the tree with its roots means that the kingdom will be restored to you when you acknowledge that Heaven rules. [27]Therefore, O king, be pleased to accept my advice: Renounce your sins by doing what is right, and your wickedness by being kind to the oppressed. It may be that then your prosperity will continue.'

Daniel identifies the decree of 'the watchers and the holy ones' with the decree of the 'Most High' and thus emphasises the ultimate authority. Once again as Nebuchadnezzar had been identified with the head of gold (2:38) now he is identified with the tree. The interpretation further shows the link between divine judgment and human responsibility. The decree is certain but the king's response can avert further judgment. Announcements of judgment are given to elicit turning to God. Nebuchadnezzar has to learn that though he may be the tree towering over and sheltering the whole earth and providing shelter to all, this power has been given and can and will easily be taken away. He will be reduced to the lowest state and will live with animals and be like them.[7]

There are to be two elements in the king's reaction. The first is an acknowledgment of God: **the Most High is sovereign in the kingdoms of men.** As an ascription of worship, Nebuchadnezzar had been ready enough to say things like this (e.g. 2:46, 4:3) but as a principle of conduct he had signally

---

[7] Nebuchadnezzar's illness is usually understood to be lycanthropy which may be associated with the rise of the legend of the werewolf. See Montgomery, pp. 220-22 and Baldwin, pp. 109-110 for further discussion.

failed to work out and live out the implications. The second is a change of lifestyle. This is not a plea for 'salvation by works', rather an evidence that he is in fact responding to the God of Daniel rather than merely giving him lip service. **What is right** was understood by later translators to mean 'almsgiving; and has been sometimes attacked as suggesting salvation by works. But this is to be simplistic. The care of the oppressed was always seen by the Hebrew prophets, especially Isaiah and Amos, as an integral part of righteousness, an emphasis particularly seen in the New Testament in the Letter of James. Such a change was needed to show that this turning to God was deeper than a mere interest or passing fancy.

The second element is the acknowledgement that the future belongs to God alone: **It may be then that your prosperity will continue**. Nebuchadnezzar still thinks that he is in control of Babylon and its destiny at least and that his greatness is unchallengeable.

The King's downfall (4:28-33)

We return to narrative and thus to the third person. But the narrative is linked directly to the dialogue by the first words of verse 28:

> [28]'All this happened to King Nebuchadnezzar. [29]Twelve months later, as the king was walking on the roof of the royal palace of Babylon, [30]he said. "Is not this the great Babylon I have built as the royal residence, by my mighty power and for the glory of my majesty?"'

There is a fine blend here of God's sovereignty and human responsibility. The dream and its interpretation in no way compelled Nebuchadnezzar to behave in this arrogant manner. Yet the dream had uncannily dramatised the king's pride and self-centredness and showed the inevitability of his behaviour given his temperament and personality. Archaeological discoveries have confirmed the massive and overwhelming splendour of ancient Babylon. Enormous walls, pierced by eight gates, and approached by magnificent streets must have been an awe-inspiring sight. Most splendid was the famous Ishtar Gate from which ran a processional highway, the scene of a splendid pageant on New Year's Day where the king accompanied the statue of Marduk in a great ceremony.[8] Doom follows swiftly.

> [31]'The words were still on his lips when a voice came from heaven, "This is what is decreed for you, King Nebuchadnezzar: Your royal authority has been taken from you. [32]You will be driven away from people and will live with the wild animals; you will eat grass like cattle. Seven times will pass by for you until you acknowledge that the Most High is sovereign over the kingdom of men and gives them to anyone he wishes."'

The voice from heaven is a deliberate contrast to the words of the king and simply overrules and indeed removes his authority. He is to experience the futility of earthly sovereignty and how utterly dependent he is on the action of God.

> [33]'Immediately what had been said about Nebuchadnezzar was fulfilled. He was driven away from people and ate grass like cattle. His body was drenched with the dew of heaven until his hair grew like the feathers of an eagle and his nails like the claws of a bird.'

To such a pathetic and ignoble state was the great king reduced. Too much time should not be spent on trying to work out the precise medical and theological symptoms; the emphasis is on the utter helplessness and humiliation of Nebuchadnezzar.

Praise and Thanksgiving (4:34-37)
We now return to the atmosphere of the first part of the chapter but with a chastened and deeper faith.

---

[8] See e.g. *Peoples of the Old Testament World,* (Baker 1994), eds. A. J. Hoerth; G. L. Mattingly; E. M. Yamauchi, especially pp. 62-64; see also *Nebuchadnezzar and Babylon,* D. J. Wiseman (O.U.P. 1987), especially pp.98-108.

³⁴'At the end of that time, I, Nebuchadnezzar, raised my eyes towards heaven, and my sanity was restored. Then I praised the Most High; I honoured and glorified him who lives for ever.

His dominion is an eternal dominion;
    his kingdom endures from generation to generation.
³⁵All the peoples of the earth
    are regarded as nothing.
He does as he pleases
    with the powers of heaven
    and the peoples of the earth.
No one can hold back his hand
    or say to him: "What have you done?" '

The phrase **at the end of that time** underlines an important theme of the book, i.e. that precise times are determined by God. In this case, when the judgment had worked, it was not needlessly prolonged. The king has learned his lesson and now, as he looks up, his reason, his well-being and his throne are restored to him. His song of praise is no conventional hymn. It springs from a new view of reality. Boasting of his own unapproachable greatness had led to him degenerating to a subhuman level. Sanity returned when he acknowledged his creatureliness. Only God's power is irresistible and enduring.

Like the previous two chapters this one ends with a return to the world of power politics but with a more realistic view of their limitations.

³⁶'At the same time that my sanity was restored, my honour and splendour were returned to me for the glory of my kingdom. My advisers and nobles sought me out, and I was restored to my throne and became even greater than before. ³⁷Now I, Nebuchadnezzar, praise and exalt and glorify the King of heaven, because everything he does is right and all his ways are just. And those who walk in pride he is able to humble.'

Only God who knows the human heart can tell how fully Nebuchadnezzar had learned his lesson. However, he has certainly

seen unmistakably the power of Daniel's God. His providence
is at work in all of human life and he is answerable to no one.
And what he does is not simply brute force, rather he is fair and
opposed to the arrogant. So this remarkable last glimpse of Nebuchadnezzar in this book ends with his warning against pride
which introduces us to a fatal example of how the proud are
humbled in Chapter 5.

General Comments
This chapter explored the relationship of human and divine power
and given us a remarkable glimpse into Nebuchadnezzar's personality. Three observations will conclude our study.

The first is that the power of God which will be fully displayed in the life of the world to come breaks into this world
from time to time. The praise coming from Nebuchadnezzar to
the 'God of heaven' is a striking reminder that even in this age
the kingdom partially comes when people acknowledge the sovereignty of God. Other Old Testament examples are Naaman in
2 Kings 5 and prophecies such as Malachi 1:11: 'My name will
be great among the nations, from the rising to the setting of the
sun. In every place incense and pure offerings will be brought
to my name...' This is a help to faith and an anticipation of the
time when 'Before me every knee will bow; by me every tongue
will swear' (Isa. 45:23 – echoed, of course, in Phil. 2:10-11).

The second point illustrated by this chapter is the interesting
blend of praise and testimony. Two things are noteworthy. The
first is that Nebuchadnezzar uses what Baldwin calls 'characteristic self-centred language'.[9] He still sees himself very much as
the centre of the universe and this is variously seen in vision as
an image or a tree and in his actions by the constructing of the
golden image. He concentrates on the signs of God in his own
life and kingdom. However, this ought not to be overdone. He
does, secondly, go beyond that to acknowledge the incomparability of the God of heaven. The praise he gives is rich and full
and is totally in line with biblical theology with its emphasis on

---

[9] Baldwin, p. 116.

the unapproachable greatness of God, his eternal plans and the unfailing nature of his providence. We do not always with all our advantages and the full revelation of God in Jesus Christ reach such heights of worship.

The third significant feature of this chapter is that it is no isolated byway but part of the highroad of biblical history, part of the Bible's plot line.[10] Nebuchadnezzar is like Adam and Eve who when confronted with another tree, instead of becoming gods, were banished from Eden. As time passes, their descendants rear a tower which is to rise to heaven. Again the result is confusion and anarchy. Yet just as here the way of pride is followed by the way of penitence and worship, so in Genesis 11 in the shadow of proud Babel, God calls Abraham to leave the city of the world and strike out into the unknown to travel to the city whose builder and architect is God. Then when the time arrives, another tree reared by human wickedness and pride becomes the way back to God. There the way up is the way down. The one who humbled himself becomes the exalted Lord to whom every knee will bow.

> So be it Lord: Thy throne shall never,
> Like earth's proud empires, pass away;
> Thy kingdom stands, and grows for ever,
> Till all thy creatures own thy sway.[11]

Questions for further study

1. Is Nebuchadnezzar a true believer by the end of this chapter?

2. What does this chapter tell us about human nature?

3. What do we learn here about God's judgment?

---

[10] See the stimulating survey in D. A. Carson, *The Gagging of God,* especially pp.193-314.

[11] 'The day thou gavest' by John Ellerton (1826-93).

5

Found wanting

I met a traveller from an antique land
Who said 'Two vast and trunkless legs of stone
Stand in the desert. Near them on the sand,
Half sunk, a shattered visage lies ....
Nothing beside remains. Round the decay
Of that colossal wreck, boundless and bare
The lone and level sands stretch far away.'[1]

These words describe the vanished empire of 'Ozymandias, King of kings' and the desolation and emptiness of the place where he had once lorded it over his minions. So it is with the empire of 'Babylon the great'. Chapter 5 of Daniel records its overthrow, never to rise again. It is a supreme irony that if the modern world knows of Babylon at all, it knows of it for the most part through the Scriptures of that despised race whom the Babylonians conquered and humiliated.

The great Nebuchadnezzar had gone, dying in 562 BC. Although the empire lasted for a little longer, its greatness was over. Without Nebuchadnezzar it had little substance: 'You are that head of gold' (2:38). It was soon to disappear, 'like chaff on a threshing floor in summer' (2:35). Belshazzar now reigned, probably as regent while his father Nabonidus was away for years on campaigns in Arabia.[2] Once again both the arrogance and fragility of human power is plainly exposed.

---

[1] From 'Ozymandias' by P. B. Shelley.
[2] For a discussion of the historicity of Belshazzar, see Introduction p. 14.

The Banquet (5:1-4)

> [1]'King Belshazzar gave a great banquet for a thousand of his no-
> bles and drank wine with them. [2]While Belshazzar was drinking
> his wine, he gave orders to bring in the gold and silver goblets that
> Nebuchadnezzar his father had taken from the temple in Jerusa-
> lem, so that the king and his nobles, his wives and his concubines
> might drink from them. [3]So they brought in the gold goblets that
> had been taken from the temple of God in Jerusalem, and the king
> and his nobles, his wives and his concubines drank from them.
> [4]As they drank the wine, they praised the gods of gold and silver,
> of bronze, iron, wood and stone.'

The narrative is fairly low-key but it has depth of association
which recall the main themes of the book. The banqueting and
wine recall the king's food and wine of Chapter 1, emphasising
the luxury of the Babylonian court and hinting at trouble to come.
As noticed in Chapter 1, there is no condemnation of wine as
such, rather it is indulgence and ostentation which is attacked.[3]
Other biblical examples of feasts which go wrong are in Esther
1 with all the consequences which flow from that, and Herod's
birthday party in Mark 6 which led to the murder of John the
Baptist.

The mention of the vessels from the temple in Jerusalem recall
the opening verses of the book and here, as the Babylonian
empire approaches its end, reminds us of the deeper meaning of
the Exile with its conflict between the God of Israel and pagan
gods. The theme of sacrilege is added to that of indulgence.
Moreover, across these opening verses of Chapter 5 falls the
ominous shadow of the closing words of Chapter 4: 'those who
walk in pride he is able to humble.' This had already happened
to Nebuchadnezzar but had led to his repentance (see further in
5:18-21). However, Belshazzar was to be humbled with no hope

---

[3] The NIV 'while Belshazzar was drinking his wine' probably means more
than simply having a drink – 'under the influence of his wine' would more
accurately bring out the meaning.

of restoration and with him was to disappear the great Babylonian empire.

This impression is reinforced by the reference to **the gods of gold and silver, of bronze, iron, wood and stone**. This reminds the reader of the inanimate nature of idols who cannot hear or respond and thus the futility of the whole Babylonian religious system. However, it also echoes the materials of the image in Chapter 2. That indicates that these gods are already judged and while their power appears to be momentarily in the ascendant the bell is already tolling for them. The scene is a warning not to be dazzled by the appearance of power and greatness but to look behind these to the reality.

The Portent (5-9)

With dreadful suddenness the God of Israel, whom Belshazzar had treated with such contempt, breaks into the drunken revelry.

> [5]Suddenly the fingers of a human hand appeared and wrote on the plaster of the wall, near the lampstand in the royal palace. The king watched the hand as it wrote. [6]His face turned pale and he was so frightened that his knees knocked together and his legs gave way.

Once again, as with the mysterious fourth figure in the furnace, we are given no explanation of this hand. Yet it remains one of the most potent and haunting images in all of literature. **Suddenly** or 'at that instant' is a phrase which has been used already in 4:33 of the suddenness of the divine judgment on Nebuchadnezzar and is another link between Chapters 4 and 5. But more than that we have, as we have noted before, a deliberate reminder that the God of the Exile is also the God of the Exodus. The hand of God which writes the doom of Babylon on the wall of the main royal audience chamber is the finger of God which was responsible for the plagues of Egypt (Exod. 8:19) and wrote the tablets of the Law, the hand which carried out judgment on all the gods of Egypt (Exod. 12:12). Once again, as with the figure in the Furnace and in the Lion's Den, there is not brute force but the awesome reality of the world beyond breaking into this one.

Faced with this Belshazzar becomes a gibbering wreck. The portent causes physical symptoms of terror and he loses control of himself. Thus, again, a man who purports to rule the world cannot rule himself. In his panic he calls for the now familiar enchanters *et al*.

> [7]The king called out for the enchanters, astrologers and diviners to be brought and said to these wise men of Babylon, 'Whoever reads this writing and tells me what it means will be clothed in purple and have a gold chain placed around his neck, and he will be made the third highest ruler in the kingdom.'

He is trying to restore his world to normality; a world where he can bestow gifts and honours and be in charge. The little detail of **the third highest ruler in the kingdom** is a striking confirmation of the historicity of the story. Belshazzar himself was number two, although exercising the powers of regent. But like all previous attempts, the efforts of the **wise men** come to nothing:

> [8]Then all the king's wise men came in, but they could not read the writing or tell the king what it meant. [9]So King Belshazzar became even more terrified and his face grew more pale. His nobles were baffled.

In a few verses the pomp and circumstance of Babylon has been reduced to helpless terror. No-one can read the writing. This does not necessarily mean that it was written in code but perhaps it was in a dialect or language they did not understand.

Daniel returns (5:10-16)

The impasse is broken by the intervention of a new character who takes charge with calm authority. This cannot be Belshazzar's queen, for his wives have already been mentioned in verse 2. Rather she is a senior and respected figure, probably the queen-mother who can remember the early years of Nebuchadnezzar's reign. It may be that the lady is in fact the wife of Nabonidus and consequently Belshazzar's mother. Thus she was perhaps the only person who could enter the royal presence uninvited.

> ¹⁰The queen, hearing the voices of the king and his nobles, came into the banquet hall. 'O king, live for ever!' she said. 'Don't be alarmed. Don't look so pale.'

However, the spotlight quickly moves from her to focus on Daniel:

> ¹¹'There is a man in your kingdom who has the spirit of the holy gods in him. In the time of your father he was found to have insight and intelligence and wisdom like that of the gods. King Nebuchadnezzar your father – your father the king, I say – appointed him chief of the magicians, enchanters, astrologers and diviners. ¹²This man Daniel, whom the king called Belteshazzar, was found to have a keen mind and knowledge and understanding, and also the ability to interpret dreams, explain riddles and solve difficult problems. Call for Daniel, and he will tell you what the writing means.'

The writer skilfully reminds us of the main thrust of the earlier chapters and how Daniel had played such a key role in Nebuchadnezzar's time. Revelation and prophetic understanding are God-given but God uses the ordinary processes of the human mind. This fits entirely with Chapter 1 where Daniel is given special understanding of dreams and visions (1:17) but also shows great diligence and application. Plainly he had been marginalised during Belshazzar's reign; he would now be in his high eighties. Once again, we have echoes of the Joseph story where Joseph is forgotten until a crisis erupts (Gen. 41:9-13).

> ¹³So Daniel was brought before the king, and the king said to him, 'Are you Daniel, one of the exiles my father the king brought from Judah? ¹⁴I have heard that the spirit of the gods is in you and that you have insight, intelligence and outstanding wisdom. ¹⁵The wise

men and enchanters were brought before me to read this writing and tell me what it means, but they could not explain it. [16]Now I have heard that you are able to give interpretations and to solve difficult problems. If you can read this writing and tell me what it means, you will be clothed in purple and have a gold chain placed around your neck, and you will be made the third highest ruler in the kingdom.'

These verses rehearse much of the earlier detail but they are not merely repetitive and underline some important principles before we come to the actual interpretation. The reference to the exiles shows that he still is reading history as if his royal power were secure and failing to realise that power is 'given'. This is reinforced by the reminder not only of Daniel's wisdom but of its divine source. Moreover, he is still seeing himself as the bestower of honours, little realising that he and his empire are on the very brink of destruction.

Daniel's Rebuke (5:17-24)
In many ways Daniel's brusqueness to Belshazzar contrasts with his earlier graciousness to Nebuchadnezzar. However, the time of judgment has come. It is too late to warn; all that remains is to announce the inevitable. In a similar vein, Amos announces the doom of Israel: 'Then the LORD said to me, "The time is ripe for my people Israel; I will spare them no longer" ' (Amos 8:2). Similarly in the book of Revelation 10:6 an angel announces 'there will be no more delay'.

[17]Then Daniel answered the king, 'You may keep your gifts for yourself and give your rewards to someone else. Nevertheless, I will read the writing for the king and tell him what it means.'

Daniel clearly wishes to avoid giving anyone the impression that divine wisdom can be bought. 'It cannot be bought with the finest gold, nor can its price be weighed in silver' (Job 28:15).

The link with Chapter 4 is now made explicit as Daniel summarises the reign of Nebuchadnezzar.

[18]'O king, the Most High God gave your father Nebuchadnezzar sovereignty and greatness and glory and splendour. [19]Because of the high position he gave him, all the peoples and nations and men of every language dreaded and feared him. Those the king wanted to put to death, he put to death; those he wanted to spare, he spared; those he wanted to promote, he promoted; and those he wanted to humble, he humbled. [20]But when his heart became arrogant and hardened with pride, he was deposed from his royal throne and stripped of his glory. [21]He was driven away from people and given the mind of an animal; he lived with the wild donkeys and ate grass like cattle; and his body was drenched with the dew of heaven, until he acknowledged that the Most High God is sovereign over the kingdoms of men and sets over them anyone he wishes.'

Daniel is doing more than giving an account of Nebuchadnezzar's reign, he is reiterating the theology of the book as a background to the fate of Belshazzar. He emphasizes the derivative nature of human power, using the word 'given' which was discussed in the commentary on Chapter 1. Yet human power is real power, and verses 19 and 20 show how 'absolute' in human sense it was. Nebuchadnezzar's mistake lay not in exercising the power which was real, but in forgetting that the power had been given him by God. This is strikingly pointed out in John 19:11 where Jesus says to Pilate: 'You would have no power over me if it were not given to you from above.' Belshazzar had been dazzled by the power and ignored the awful consequences of arrogance which for him were to be fatal.

[22]'But you his son, O Belshazzar, have not humbled yourself, though you knew all this. [23]Instead, you have set yourself up against the Lord of heaven. You had the goblets from his temple brought to you, and you and your nobles, your wives and your concubines drank wine from them. You praised the gods of silver and gold, of bronze, iron and wood and stone, which cannot see or hear or understand. But you did not honour the God who holds in his hand your life and all your ways. [24]Therefore he sent the hand that wrote the inscription.'

Every phrase rings eerily like a death sentence. Every shred of credibility is gone from the hapless Belshazzar. He may have thought he was vaunting his power over 'the god in Jerusalem' who had been so spectacularly humiliated by the gods of Babylon. Rather like Pharaoh and Sennacherib he had challenged 'the Lord of heaven', the Creator who controlled his breath and 'his ways', and now he was lurching to an inglorious end. The hand which wrote on the wall was a visible expression of that power Belshazzar had tried to defy.

The Interpretation (5:25-28)

Suspense has built up steadily but only now, when we know clearly what the issues are, is the inscription revealed:

> 25'This in the inscription that was written:
>   MENE, MENE, MENE, TEKEL, PARSIN

The words, although they sound strange to us, would not have done so to readers of Hebrew and Aramaic. Rather they have a straightforward surface meaning which refers to three weights. Goldingay usefully points out that the 'inscription thus represents something like a merchant's shout: "Reckoned at a mina, a shekel, and 'two halves!' " or his documentary record of this evaluation.'[4] However, it needs Daniel to interpret the inner significance of the words. Just as dreams and visions are not self-explanatory, so this inscription needs to be expounded. Significantly Daniel takes the verbal roots rather than the nouns and thus shows that God's assessments and judgments were dynamic rather than static.

> 26'This is what these words mean:
>   Mene: God has numbered the days of your reign and
>   brought it to an end.
> 27Tekel: You have been weighed on the scales and found
>   wanting.
> 28Peres: Your kingdom is divided and given to the Medes
>   and Persians.'

---

[4] Goldingay, p. 111.

As we shall see, particularly in Chapter 7, there is an inevitable tension between the sovereign guiding of history by God and the freedom of human agents to act, but a careful examination of what the text says shows a fine balance between the two. The first statement, interpreting 'Mene' is a specific illustration of the general theology of the book that **the Most High God is Sovereign over the kingdoms of men** (v. 21). Yet during that reign Belshazzar could have acted differently from the way he did and was in no way compelled to act in a godless way.

This is confirmed by the interpretation of 'Tekel'. The weighing on the scales suggests a just judgment being imposed; **found wanting** implies that it is not a foregone conclusion. Perhaps this may be one of the passages which lies behind the awesome picture of the Final Judgment in Revelation 20:15: 'If anyone's name was not found written in the book of life, he was thrown into the lake of fire.'

All this leads to the inevitable historical consequence: a divided and conquered kingdom. Here the wordplay on 'Peres' allows Daniel to mention that kingdom which would be the immediate cause of Babylon's downfall. But the alert reader will have noticed the now familiar phrase 'given'. Media/Persia may be the agent but they are acting only as agents of the God of heaven to whom power belongs. Thus this marks another stage on the road to the kingdom which was to be a great mountain filling the whole earth.

The Aftermath (5:29-31)
In a manner we have come to recognise as typical of our author the chapter ends with a historical note where Belshazzar's last command is deliberately juxtaposed with his violent death.

> [29]Then at Belshazzar's command, Daniel was clothed in purple, a gold chain was placed around his neck, and he was proclaimed the third highest ruler in the kingdom.
> [30]That very night Belshazzar, king of the Babylonians, was slain, [31]and Darius the Mede took over the kingdom, at the age of sixty-two.

It is a grim irony that Belshazzar's command is carried out only for him to be almost immediately removed from the possibility of ever giving any other orders. **That very night** underlines the swiftness and certainty of the judgment. The language is terse and matter of fact sounding, much more like historical data than legend. The mention of the age of **Darius the Mede** is one of such little details which read like specific information of a particular person. Thus, unlamented and unloved, the Babylonian empire passes into history and a new empire now emerges on the centre of the stage.

General Comments
It might be useful to sum up the message of the chapter by making four observations:

1. Belshazzar is not depicted as excessively wicked, rather he comes across as vain and headstrong. He is guilty of that most basic sin of arrogance, of failing to take into account the God who held his very life in his hands. His story is like that of the rich fool in Luke 12:20 to whom God said, 'This very night your life will be demanded from you.' Both are fools in the biblical sense of taking no account of God (see Ps. 14:1). Thus the chapter is a salutary reminder to 'number our days' (Ps. 90:12), and a warning against a practical atheism.

2. The author is continuing to make shrewd comments on the nature of power politics. Once again we have the whole panoply of state at a function and once again it is reduced to helplessness. This time, unlike Nebuchadnezzar in Chapters 3 and 4, Belshazzar acts far too late; the time is ripe for a change, the tide of history is flowing fast against him.

3. The divine control of history does not simply override human beings, as we shall explore more fully in Chapter 7. Rather human behaviour is one of the factors God takes into account in his overall ordering of events. There is always a choice. It is always

possible to behave differently. This is well illustrated in this chapter by the calm and responsible intervention of the queen mother. Every day and every circumstance brings its choices which call for a response which will either be for God and blessing or against him and lead to destruction.

4. A final comment is that the Divine voice cannot be silenced. For a long time Daniel's role had been in the shadows as he was marginalised at Belshazzar's court. But when the time came, his was the only voice which would speak with authority and reveal once again the voice of God.

Questions for further study

1. Why did Daniel not call Belshazzar to repent?

2. What sin did Belshazzar commit?

3. If you were giving an evangelistic talk based on this chapter, what kind of things would you say?

6

Shut the mouths of lions

Even in these days of minimal knowledge of the Bible, the story of Daniel in the Lion's Den is probably still reasonably familiar. However, what we must try to do is to set the chapter in context, standing as it does at the end of the first part of the book and summing up the stories before plunging into the Apocalyptic chapters. The story here underlines and carries forward many of the themes and motifs of the earlier chapters. It completes the historical record of Daniel and his activities: 1:21 has spoken of his career lasting until the first year of Cyrus, and 6:28 reminds us of that. In many respects it recalls the story of the Blazing Furnace in Chapter 3 but, as we shall see, it is no mere repetition of that earlier story. We shall look at the chapter as it develops in four stages:

The New Régime (6:1-3)
Daniel, as Chapter 1 had predicted, continues to enjoy a position of influence, although now an old man, probably in his eighties. The vigour and efficiency of the new régime contrast vividly with the decadence of the previous one.

> [1]It pleased Darius to appoint 120 satraps to rule throughout the kingdom, [2]with three administrators over them, one of whom was Daniel. The satraps were made accountable to them so that the king might not suffer loss. [3]Now Daniel so distinguished himself among the administrators and the satraps by his exceptional qualities that the king planned to set him over the whole kingdom.

The key phrase is **that the king might not suffer loss**. It is always a preoccupation of governments to establish sound finances. Daniel's role in all this is a salutary reminder that this

85

most visionary of men is also practical, efficient and has his feet firmly on the ground. Commentators make much of the fact that the **three administrators** are not mentioned elsewhere, but the main point of the allusion here is to tell us Daniel's specific position. As is customary in this book, the historical details have a precision which suggests accurate information and reminiscence rather than vaguely understood background.

The Plot (6:4-15)

These new arrangements, however, made Daniel the target of jealousy and his fellow officials plot his destruction.

> [4]At this, the administrators and the satraps tried to find grounds for charges against Daniel in his conduct of government affairs, but they were unable to do so. They could find no corruption in him, because he was trustworthy and neither corrupt nor negligent. [5]Finally these men said, 'We will never find any basis for charges against this man Daniel unless it has something to do with the law of his God.'

Behind these laconic verses lies a whole world of intrigue and skulduggery. Daniel's every movement would be watched by an army of spies, his every word would be analysed and yet **they could find no corruption in him**. Eventually they decide to target **something to do with the law of his God**. Once again the spectre of the state demanding absolute allegiance is rearing its head, as in Chapter 3. It is a necessary reminder that the life of faith must be lived to the very end and that earlier victories and rescues cannot be taken as guarantees of absence of future crises. Moreover, the leisureliness of the narrative builds up suspense. A sinister plot is hatched and a trap sprung.

> [6]So the administrators and satraps went as a group to the king and said, 'O King Darius, live for ever! [7]The royal administrators, prefects, satraps, advisers and governors have all agreed that the king should issue an edict and enforce the decree that anyone who prays to any god or man during the next thirty days, except to you, O

king, shall be thrown into the lions' den. ⁸Now, O king, issue the
decree and put it in writing so that it cannot be altered – in accordance with the laws of the Medes and the Persians which cannot be
repealed.' ⁹So King Darius put the decree in writing.

As in Chapter 3 we have the sense of self-importance and
overbearing power implied in the roll-call of names. This is a
blatant exercise of collective power and intimidation. We can
only speculate as to why the king agreed to this rather bizarre
request. Perhaps as a relatively new monarch he did not wish to
antagonise the whole body of officials, although he must have
wondered why Daniel was not part of his deputation. It may be,
however, that he simply thought the request was so odd that it
was unlikely ever to be implemented. In any case the interest
now focuses on how Daniel will respond.

¹⁰Now when Daniel learned that the decree had been published, he
went home to his upstairs room where the windows opened towards Jerusalem. Three times a day he got down on his knees and
prayed, giving thanks to his God, just as he had done before. ¹¹Then
these men went as a group and found Daniel praying and asking
God for help.

It would be a misunderstanding to see this as mandatory for
ways and times of praying, although three times a day at morning,
noon and evening reflects the concern to give the whole day to
God. Jerusalem was currently in ruins and praying towards it
was a statement of faith that it would be restored. That was a
statement of belief that God, the Lord of history, who had set
his name there would never finally abandon it. Nor was this
exceptional behaviour – **just as he had done before**.

Verse 11 confirms that Daniel's whole attitude is one of
dependence and trust – **asking God for help**. This is not the
first time Daniel had done so. In 2:17 ff. he and his friends had
prayed that God would reveal to them both Nebuchadnezzar's
dream and how to interpret it. There that prayer had been fully
answered and this helps to strengthen Daniel in this situation.

The power of the state is, however, about to move into action:

> [12]So they went to the king and spoke to him about his royal decree:
> 'Did you not publish a decree that during the next thirty days any-
> one who prays to any god or man except to you, O king, would be
> thrown into the lions' den?'
>
> The king answered, 'The decree stands – in accordance with
> the laws of the Medes and Persians which cannot be repealed.'
>
> [13]Then they said to the king, 'Daniel, who is one of the exiles
> from Judah, pays no attention to you, O king, or to the decree you
> put in writing. He still prays three times a day.' [14]When the king
> heard this, he was greatly distressed; he was determined to rescue
> Daniel and made every effort until sundown to save him.
>
> [15]Then the men went as a group to the king and said to him,
> 'Remember, O king, that according to the law of the Medes and
> Persians no decree or edict that the king issues can be changed.'

With a few clear strokes the author has again sketched both the
terror and the limitations of human power. Once again, as in
Chapter 3, the state is claiming godlike power and thus
demanding absolute obedience. Yet the perpetrators of this state
of affairs cower together for security and Darius, absolute
monarch as he is, cannot act bravely because of public opinion.
So it was with Herod Antipas and John the Baptist, and with
Pontius Pilate and Jesus. All through these chapters we have
been reminded of the provisional and temporary nature of human
power as well as its ferociousness and arbitrary nature.

Daniel, as he had done in those long past days of youth in
Chapter 1, takes his stand with firmness and courage. He is now
a man in his eighties but has stood firm all those long years. But
above all, this chapter is giving us one of the clearest Old
Testament windows into Christ himself. He too was the victim
of intrigue and it was as he prayed in Gethsemane he was arrested.
Efforts were made to rescue him and, as we shall see, he too
went down into the den and apparent defeat. Yet, unlike Daniel,
he is also the one whose kingdom will replace all human
kingdoms and will fulfil all the prophecies of this ancient book.

However, at this moment, all seems to be lost and, as in Chapter 3, the state juggernaut rolls on to crush opposition.

The Den (6:16-24)
The story is told with restraint and economy of detail but is full of suspense and builds up to a nail-biting climax.

> [16]So the king gave the order, and they brought Daniel and threw him into the lions' den. The king said to Daniel, 'May your God whom you serve continually, rescue you.'

The contrast with 3:15 is striking at this point. There Nebuchadnezzar had boasted: 'What god will be able to rescue you from my hand?' Here Darius practically anticipates the outcome of the story and so realises clearly the issues involved. Nebuchadnezzar had looked only at the physical and human realities in the situation and had failed to perceive the greater reality beyond. Here Darius, already acutely aware of the limitations of his own apparently absolute power, virtually appeals to a greater power. Indeed, arguably he himself breaks his own law, for his words in verse 16 are in fact a heartfelt prayer.[1]

However, as in Chapter 3, there appears to be no way out of a grisly fate and once again the story teller uses circumstantial detail to emphasise the hopelessness of Daniel's plight.

> [17]A stone was brought and placed over the mouth of the den, and the king sealed it with his own signet ring and with the rings of his nobles, so that Daniel's situation might not be changed. [18]Then the king returned to his palace and spent the night without eating and without any entertainment being brought to him. And he could not sleep.

The stone makes physical rescue extremely difficult and the sealing makes it a capital offence to disturb. Darius, however,

---

[1] Indeed Darius' words are actually a stronger affirmation, for the Aramaic word more properly should be translated '*will* save you', the NIV, following the RSV, weakens the sense.

cannot eat, divert himself or sleep and spends the night in an agony of suspense.

> [19]At the first light of dawn, the king got up and hurried to the lions' den. [20]When he came near the den, he called to Daniel in an anguished voice, 'Daniel, servant of the living God, has your God, whom you serve continually, been able to rescue you from the lions?'

There is no pomp and circumstance here, no attempt to preserve royal dignity; Darius hurries frantically to the den. Significantly he uses that most characteristic Old Testament title, **living God**, i.e. not just the God who is alive but the God who gives life and is continually active. In Deuteronomy 5:26 it is the living God who speaks out of the fire at Sinai; in Joshua 3:10 it is the living God who drives out Israel's enemies; in 1 Samuel 17:26 David uses this name against Goliath; and in 2 Kings 19:4 Hezekiah invokes this God against the Assyrians. This immediately creates an expectation of something significant and again reduces the power of the state to impotence. The phrase, **whom you serve continually**, is a fine summary of what has been the consuming passion of Daniel's life.

> [21]Daniel answered, 'O king, live for ever! [22]My God sent his angel, and he shut the mouths of the lions. They have not hurt me, because I was found innocent in his sight. Nor have I ever done any wrong before you, O king.'

As always there is no explanation of the 'mechanics' of the rescue. Angels play a prominent role in the defence of God's people and this is usually simply stated as a fact. Daniel shows his characteristic politeness by using the phrase, **O king, live for ever** – the first time this address has been used by Daniel or his friends. The king is in no danger of being arrogant about titles after the experience he has been through. Daniel was **innocent**, a legal word implying that God vindicated the integrity of his servant. Similarly the attempt to discredit him with the king, which had been the object of the plot, had also totally failed. He had put loyalty to God first and this had also meant a more true loyalty to the state than could otherwise have happened.

Events now move swiftly and the conspirators are engulfed in the fate they had planned for Daniel.

> [23]The king was overjoyed and gave orders to lift Daniel out of the den. And when Daniel was lifted from the den, no wound was found on him, because he had trusted in his God.
> [24]At the king's command, the men who had falsely accused Daniel were brought in and thrown into the lions' den, along with their wives and children. And before they reached the floor of the den, the lions overpowered them and crushed all their bones.

Just as, on emerging from the furnace, the three friends had not even a smell of burning, so Daniel does not even have a scratch. Probably it is the incident which the author of Hebrews has in mind when he speaks of those who by faith 'shut the mouths of lions' (Heb. 11:33). We shall explore further the relationship of prayer and the sovereignty of God in Chapter 10.

The grisly fate of the conspirators and their families is recorded without comment. It would be wrong to see it as an example of gloating rather than a sober realisation of the reality of judgment in the world. The king's judgment may have been harsh, but God in his overarching providence makes everything work out his will. Even though there may be sinfulness and cruelty in the human actors, God's ultimate purposes are just and loving.

The Song of Praise (6:25-28)

In Chapters 2, 3 and 4, Nebuchadnezzar had praised Daniel's God in an increasingly reverent way. In Chapter 5 there had been no such praise from Belshazzar who had already passed the point of no return. Here Darius virtually encapsulates the theology of the whole book in a song of praise which summarises what God has done in the last chapters and points forward to the theology of history about to be unfolded in the second part of the book.

> [25]Then King Darius wrote to all the peoples, nations and men of every language throughout the land:
> 'May you prosper greatly!
> [26]'I issue a decree that in every part of my kingdom people must fear and reverence the God of Daniel.

> For he is the living God
>   and he endures for ever;
> his kingdom will not be destroyed,
>   his dominion will never end.
> [27]He rescues and he saves,
>   he performs signs and wonders
>   in the heavens and on the earth.
> He has rescued Daniel
>   from the power of the lions.'

Once again the universal nature of this God who controls **all the peoples** is emphasised. The song of praise could have come straight from the Psalter and is again a sign of the godly influence of Daniel.

Goldingay[2] points out the resemblance to Psalm 2 where the plots of the nations have been frustrated and God's king is established. This reminds us of the overruling providence of God which is to be one of the main themes of Chapters 7–12. Moreover, it is more than generalised tributes of praise; the specific case of Daniel's rescue from the lions shows that God's power is practical and can be demonstrated in this world.

A historical note concludes this chapter and with its echo of 1:21 rounds off this first half of the book.

> [28]So Daniel prospered during the reign of Darius and the reign of Cyrus the Persian.

---

[2] Goldingay, p. 136.

Reasons have already been given[3] for taking 'Darius' and 'Cyrus' as alternative names for the king elsewhere usually simply known as 'Cyrus'. This would mean that 'and' here has the sense of 'namely'. In any case the reminder of Daniel's witness in the court for the better part of seventy years is a tribute both to God's faithfulness and his own integrity.

General Comments

Four observations will help us to gain an overview of this chapter.

1. Chapter 6, like 1–5 has explored the theme of power and its limitations. Even an absolute monarch is constrained both by his court and by his own conscience. Only God rules without either the constraints of time or of having to give an account to anyone. Yet this is no arbitrary exercise of unchallenged power; God, in his grace, allows humans to co-operate with him. He 'gives' authority. We looked at this important word in Chapter 1 and will examine it again in Chapter 7. Also he listens to his servants and this is to raise the second main issue.

2. The importance of prayer is underlined here. The value of regular prayer times and places, although not an absolute pattern to follow, remains a vital part of praying. Perhaps here a major interest is in the relationship of the prayer and the angel (not dissimilar to Peter's rescue from prison in Acts 12). More of this is part of the thrust of Chapter 10. Prayer already played a significant part in the events of Chapter 2.

3. As in Chapter 3 we have a miraculous rescue. This does not mean, as it did not mean in Chapter 3, that God's people will always be rescued from the fury of the flames and the jaws of the lions. What it does mean is that from time to time, even in this world, God reveals that power of his kingdom which is to characterise the age to come. Because of that, God's people can

---

[3] See Introduction, pp. 14-15.

confidently look to vindication in a life beyond this one even though they may be destroyed in this one. When many early Christians faced the violence of lions in the arena, no angel intervened, yet they faced death in the confidence that Jesus, not Caesar was Lord, and that he would have the last word.

4. And that is the fourth point. This story foreshadows something greater. Jesus, like Daniel, was falsely accused by a powerful clique of conspirators. Like Daniel he was condemned. Unlike Daniel no angel appeared to prevent his going to the Cross. Yet because he not only was the innocent victim like Daniel, but the everlasting king of whom Daniel speaks, the Son of Man coming with the clouds of heaven, angels appear at another pit. Another stone is rolled away and death is rendered impotent.

> Thine be the glory, risen conquering Son,
> Endless is the victory, thou o'er death hast won;
> Angels in bright raiment rolled the stone away,
> Kept the folded grave clothes where thy body lay.[4]

Questions for further study

1. Should Daniel's practice of prayer be used as a pattern?

2. Compare and contrast this incident with Chapter 3.

3. Why is God called 'the living God?'

---

[4] 'Thine be the glory' by Edmond Budry (1854-1932).

cc

7

Your kingdom come

We move now in Daniel 7 to a type of literature which resembles in many ways science fiction which, especially with modern film techniques and 'virtual reality', transports us to distant galaxies and other dimensions. In the introduction some comments were made on Apocalyptic,[1] but a few words would not be out of place here. This vast body of literature, including also Zechariah and Revelation, has its own conventions, symbols and vocabulary. One particular convention is the use of symbolic numbers: 4 is the number of the earth and 10 stands for a large but unspecified number.

Numbers had a particular fascination for apocalyptic writers and essentially spring from the conviction that all time and space is providentially ordered by God, particularly as illustrated in the seven days of creation. Four rivers run out of Eden, and these symbolise the life giving presence of God flowing to the four corners of the earth. Thus numbers are part of the meaning.

Apocalyptic looks beyond the actual events and personalities of history and sees these as manifestations of great spiritual realities and the age-long struggle of good and evil. The veil, through which we have caught glimpses in earlier chapters, is now torn aside and we are shown the essence of both divine and human power. The whole sweep of history is covered from creation to final judgment. In every sense this chapter is the hinge of the book; later chapters treat part of the picture but this goes right to the heart of the nature of the earthly and heavenly kingdoms. The Aramaic continues, thus linking it with Chapters 2–6.[2]

---

[1] See Introduction, pp. 16-17.
[2] On the Aramaic of Daniel see Introduction, p. 15.

The scene set (7:1)

> In the first year of Belshazzar King of Babylon, Daniel had a dream, and visions passed through his mind as he was lying on his bed. He wrote down the substance of his dream.

The time is important. **The first year of Belshazzar** places it between Chapters 4 and 5. We noticed in the discussion of Chapter 5 how Daniel had been marginalised at Belshazzar's court. He has not, however, been marginalised by God and this vision shows that the God revealed in the stories of Chapters 1–6 is in control and that what he does is valid to all eternity. **He wrote down ... the dream** shows Daniel's consciousness of the importance of the subject and the need to preserve it for others to read.

The Vision of the Beasts from the sea (7:2-8)

> ²Daniel said: 'In my vision at night I looked, and there before me were the four winds of heaven churning up the great sea. ³Four great beasts, each different from the others, came up out of the sea.'

The **four winds of heaven** are the four main winds blowing from the main points of the compass and are mentioned in the Babylonian creation myth.[3] However, it seems likely that 'the four winds' are a deliberate echo of Genesis 1:2 where the Spirit of God swoops[4] over the waters. It is thus a powerful reminder that the Creator is in charge of the processes of history. This is further emphasised by the use of the verb 'given', already noted in Chapter 1 (see verses 4 and 6).

Daniel here is seeing both the origin and the nature of human power. The beasts come up from **the great sea**. Firstly, this has a geographical meaning i.e. the Mediterranean. Joshua 1:4

---

[3] In the Babylonian Text – *The Seven Tablets of Creation*.
[4] The word 'swoops' is a better translation than 'brooded' or 'hovered'. The participle *merahepet* is used in Deuteronomy 32:11 of eagles swooping, and suggests the vigour of God's creation.

mentions the 'Great Sea' as the western boundary of the promised
land. Power is shifting westwards away from the old empires of
Babylonia and Persia and towards the rising powers of Greece
and Rome. Secondly, there is the sense of the raging powers of
the nations; see e.g. Isaiah 17:12: 'Oh the raging of many nations
– they rage like the raging sea!'; also in Revelation 17:15: 'the
waters you saw, where the prostitute sits, are peoples, multitudes,
nations and languages.' The raging sea of the nations keeps on
throwing up power-hungry régimes. Thirdly, the sea is the
symbol of supernatural evil, the primaeval deep, the haunt of
the monster Leviathan; see, for example, Job 41:31; Psalm 74:12-
14; and in Revelation 13:1 the beast, at the instigation of the
dragon, rises out of the sea.

Thus Daniel, in a few swift strokes, shows us the origin of
human power. Specific régimes arise in real geographical areas
at actual times. Yet these are also illustrative of the general tur-
bulence and flux of human society from which new powers are
continually emerging. Yet behind all this is the sinister influence of spirit powers of which we are to be given another glimpse
in Chapter 10. But more fundamental still, behind all these other
influences stands the power of **the Most High** who ultimately
uses all human power to work out his will.

The other introductory issue is, what régimes do these four
beasts represent? The answer to this depends usually on the
commentator's view of when the book was written. If we take
the majority view, the four empires are Babylon, Media, Persia
and Greece. This view, as we saw in the introduction,[5] places
the book in the second century, and sees it as a response to the
tyranny of Antiochus Epiphanes, reading it as history rather than
predictive prophecy. The second view, defended by some
significant scholars, is that the book was in fact a product of the
Exile or immediate post-Exilic period and that the four empires
are Babylon, Persia, Greece and Rome. I have already given
reasons for accepting that view and shall comment further in
Chapter 11. However, it is vital not to get side-tracked into

regarding this as the most important issue. What is vital is that
here we have divine commentary on the nature and course of
human history and régimes which arise again and again.
Revelation 17:8 speaks of the beast who 'once was, now is not,
and yet will come'.

> 4'The first was like a lion, and it had the wings of an eagle. I watched
> until its wings were torn off and it was lifted from the ground so
> that it stood on two feet like a man, and the heart of a man was
> given to it.'

We must first remember that comparing people and nations to
creatures is a common phenomenon. Britain, in the days of
empire, was often compared to a lion. The Russian bear and the
American eagle are other examples. The suggestion is that
communities and régimes take on a character of their own which
is symbolised by various creatures.

The first beast combines the majesty and ferocity of the lion
and the swiftness of the eagle. In Jeremiah 49:19-22 they are
used to describe Nebuchadnezzar, and none of the interpretations
doubt that this first beast is Babylon, the empire in which the
stories and visions are set. They represent the swift and ruthless
way in which Nebuchadnezzar destroyed the Assyrian empire
and numerous petty kingdoms including Judah. A winged lion
with a man's head was discovered in excavations at the ancient
city of Nimrud, showing this was a symbol well known to the
Babylonians. The plucking of its wings and subsequent human
like behaviour recalls Chapter 4 with Nebuchadnezzar's humiliation and restoration. On the other hand, 'the heart (or mind) of
a man' points to something more cultured and constructive and
reminds us of the undoubted intellectual and cultural advances of
this empire (which Daniel experienced in Chapter 1).

> 5'And there before me was a second beast, which looked like a
> bear. It was raised up on one of its sides, and it had three ribs in its
> mouth between its teeth. It was told, "Get up and eat your fill of
> flesh."'

This second beast has the lumbering power and ravenous appetite of a bear which is encouraged to indulge its predatory instincts. Whether the three ribs have any precise significance is doubtful:[6] **It was told**; the speaker is presumably God himself or a member of the Divine court, a reminder of the providence behind the rise of this great empire.

> [6]'After that, I looked, and there before me was another beast, one that looked like a leopard. And on its back it had four wings like those of a bird. This beast had four heads, and it was given authority to rule.'

This animal was notable for its speed and agility. The four heads suggest the universal scope of this empire and could also represent the four divisions of the Greek empire after the death of Alexander the Great. Like the first two beasts, **it was given authority**; its power was not autonomous. The universal dominion of this third power is also mentioned in the parallel passage in 2:39: 'a third kingdom ... will rule over the whole earth.'

> [7]'After that, in my vision at night I looked, and there before me was a fourth beast – terrifying and frightening and very powerful. It had large iron teeth; it crushed and devoured its victims and trampled underfoot whatever was left. It was different from all the former beasts and it had ten horns.'

Once again the **large iron teeth** link it with the fourth kingdom of 2:40: 'there will be a fourth kingdom, strong as iron.' This beast is not identifiable; like Behemoth and Leviathan in Job 40 and 41 it has characteristics of other beasts but is greater than the sum of its parts. It initially, I believe, represents Rome with its massive military conquests. The beast from the sea in Revelation 13:1-2 is based on this, with added features from the first three. Similarly the great prostitute of Revelation 17 rides

---

[6] E. J. Young in *Daniel* (Banner of Truth Trust, Edinburgh, 1972) says it probably refers to Babylon, Lydia and Egypt, p. 145.

on the beast with ten horns. In these cases the primary reference is to the persecuting Roman empire. However, neither here nor in Revelation does this exhaust the meaning of the beast.

This fourth apparition is **different from all the former beasts**. This is the evil power of militarism and oppression in every generation. Not all human power is bad; there are cultural, scientific and humanitarian advances in most periods of history. Here, however, is unbridled ambition, devilish cruelty and overbearing arrogance. This is an important reminder of how to read Apocalyptic. I have already argued that we have here an unfolding of history and that the four beasts represent Babylon, Persia, Greece and Rome. This does not mean that this is the only significance of the passage. The meaning is not only chronological but moral and spiritual. It would be hard to argue that Rome *per se* was more wicked and cruel than the other régimes. Rather a deeper point is being made.

Rome was the régime in power when the 'Prince of princes' (8:25) came to earth and started to build that kingdom which was the rock that destroyed the image (2:44-45). In the clash of Rome and the church, of Caesar and Christ, the events foretold in Daniel begin to unfold. Thus Rome represents that power opposed to God which surfaces in every generation. This is the point of the ten horns who are the ten kings (v. 24). More will be said in the comments on verses 23ff. Ten is a number suggesting completeness.[7] This evil power of militarism has surfaced horribly in our own generation, especially in the two great World Wars and, at the time of writing, in recent horrors in Bosnia and Central Africa.

> [8] 'While I was thinking about the horns, there before me was another horn, a little one, which came up among them; and three of the first horns were uprooted before it. This horn had eyes like the eyes of a man and a mouth that spoke boastfully.'

The horn is a symbol of power, for example, in another apoca-

[7] See Goldingay, p. 164.

lyptic work, Zechariah 1:18-20, four horns scatter Israel. In Deuteronomy 33:17 Joseph is described as having 'horns of a wild ox', with which he will subdue the nations. This horn has those human features which suggest authority. The eyes here are probably the proud looks of 'the eyes of the arrogant man' (Isa. 2:11). This is underlined by **the mouth that spoke boast-fully**. This will be further explained in verse 25. I shall reserve comment on the identity of the **little horn** for the later part of the chapter where the interpretation is given.

The Thrones in Heaven (7:9-18)

The seer has been given an awesome glimpse of the reality of devilish and human power. Now the perspective switches and another reality becomes apparent; the throne of God towering above the raging nations.

> 9'As I looked,
>
> thrones were set in place,
>   and the Ancient of Days took his seat.
> His clothing was as white as snow,
>   the hair of his head was white like wool.
> His throne was flaming with fire,
>   and its wheels were all ablaze.
> 10A river of fire was flowing,
>   coming out from before him.
> Thousands upon thousands attended him,
>   ten thousands times ten thousand stood before him.
> The court was seated,
>   and the books were opened.'

In contrast to the fury and aggression of the previous scene, this one is of calmness, light and ultimate sovereignty. It draws on other passages but has woven these references into a beautiful poem which becomes the model for similar passages, especially in the book of Revelation. The idea of the heavenly court is a familiar one in the Old Testament. 1 Kings 22:19ff. records the vision of the prophet Micaiah ben Imlah who sees 'the LORD

sitting on his throne with all the host of heaven standing around
him on his right and on his left'. Similarly in Isaiah 6:8: 'who
will go for us?' shows the presence of others in the court of
heaven.

But an important point is implied here. Many thrones **were
set in place** and are presumably occupied by members of the
heavenly court. This is paralleled in Revelation 4:4 where the
twenty-four elders sit on thrones. Yet there, as here, the focus is
on the central throne and 'him who sits on the throne' (Rev.
4:10). So here, while many thrones are placed and later the court
is seated, one alone is the centre and he sits first.

The one who sits is described as **the Ancient of Days** and
this suggests that his reign, unlike that of the beasts, is not limited
in time. Similar expressions occur in the Psalter, for example:
'You, O God, are my king from of old' (74:12); 'from everlasting
to everlasting you are God' (90:2). He 'takes his seat' as of right.

There follows a highly symbolic description of the 'Ancient
of Days'. The whiteness of his clothes and hair suggests purity
and the fact that his power is exercised with integrity and justice.
There are no stains on his character. So in Revelation 1:14 the
Risen Lord appears with 'head and hair ... white like wool, as
white as snow'.

The next symbol is that of fire, regularly used as the sign of
the immediate presence of God in judgment and in mercy. At
the gates of Eden burns a flaming sword (Gen. 3:24); God appears
in flames of fire (Exod. 3:2); Jesus will baptise with the Holy
Spirit and fire (Matt. 3:11). These are a few of the many biblical
examples. **Its wheels were all ablaze** and **a river of fire was
flowing** suggests that not only is this throne stable but also it is
characterised by active dynamism. A similar idea is found in
Psalm 97:3: 'Fire goes before him and consumes his foes on
every side.'

Around this awesome throne stand **thousands upon thousands** and **ten thousand times ten thousand**. Again similar
ideas occur elsewhere. Psalm 89:5 speaks of 'the assembly of
the holy ones'. Then books are opened, which obviously again

is part of the picture of the court in session. The idea of a record in heaven is again a familiar one and makes its final appearance in Revelation 20:12 when at the final assize before the Great White Throne the books are opened and judgment pronounced accordingly. Thus here as well the emphasis is on the fairness of the judgment.

In the manner of dreams and visions, where scenes dissolve into each other without logical connections, we return to the little horn and the fate of the fourth beast.

> [11]'Then I continued to watch because of the boastful words the horn was speaking. I kept looking until the beast was slain and its body destroyed and thrown into the blazing fire. [12](The other beasts had been stripped of their authority, but were allowed to live for a period of time.)'

This is the carrying out of the divine sentence on particularly the fourth beast which is consumed by the blazing fire coming from the throne. So in Revelation 20:14-15 those judged are 'thrown into the lake of fire'. How and when this happens is not specified; simply the reality of judgment is emphasised.

Verse 12 reminds us again of the importance of not simply reading these details in a flat linear way. If the slaying of the beast points to the destruction of evil at the end of the age (and it does), it is also important to remember that this court sits permanently and its judgments are always present in history. So it is that many nations continue in a reduced form long after their days of greatness are gone.

Yet the vision does not end there. A new and significant figure is introduced:

> [13]'In my vision at night, I looked, and there before me was one like a son of man, coming with the clouds of heaven. He approached the Ancient of Days and was led into his presence. [14]He was given authority, glory and sovereign power; all peoples, nations and men of every language worshipped him. His dominion is an everlasting dominion that will not pass away, and his kingdom is one that will never be destroyed.'

This passage is one of the great moments of Old Testament revelation and a vast amount of commentary has been devoted to it.[8] A number of introductory comments need to be made. The first is that this figure comes **with the clouds of heaven**. The beasts have risen from the sea, an integral part of both the geographical and metaphorical world order. This figure comes from outside that order but is intimately linked with it. The clouds echo the glory of the Lord which appeared in a cloud in Exodus 16:10. Then in Deuteronomy 33:26 God 'rides on the heavens to help you and on the clouds in his majesty'. In Psalm 68:4, he 'rides on the clouds', and in Psalm 104:3, 'He makes the clouds his chariot and rides on the wings of the wind.' Thus the unique link of this figure with God is emphasised. Moreover, the context of these other passages is of God's providence, guidance and help, and thus the strong suggestion is that the earthly powers are to be ruled by someone who comes from outside them.

The second comment is a word on the phrase translated **like a son of man**. It means 'like a human being' and is an echo of earlier phrases such as 'like a lion' (v. 4), and thus is intended to stand against these earlier figures. The Hebrew phrases occur sometimes in parallel with the more ordinary word for 'human', for example, Psalm 8:4: 'What is man that you are mindful of him, the son of man that you care for him?' or Job 25:6: 'Man, who is but a maggot – a son of man, who is only a worm?' It is used ninety-three times in Ezekiel as a form of address to the prophet, and indeed Daniel himself is so addressed in 8:17. Does this mean, as many commentators have argued, that a Messianic interpretation is ruled out and that such a view was read back into it by later generations?

We must, I believe, link this with the general teaching of the Bible on humanity, and particularly on humanity as the image of God and the subsequent command to have dominion over the earth (Gen. 1:26). This was later lost by the Fall which resulted

---

[8] A standard book which treats the subject exhaustively is *Son of Man* (SPCK 1979) by M. Casey. Useful summaries can be found in Goldingay, pp. 169-172 and Baldwin, pp. 148-154.

in the proliferation of beast-like régimes and the rule of the earth by naked power seen here in vision and illustrated in Chapters 1–6. Thus this chapter is an important stage in the development of the story line of the Bible, pointing as it does to the renewal and restoration of the whole of creation by someone who both comes from heaven and is intimately related to humanity.

Yet in verse 27 (of which more later) the kingdom is said to be given **to the saints, the people of the Most High**. Because of this some commentators argue that the Son of Man cannot be a personal figure but must be a symbol of the Jewish people, or at least a favoured remnant among them. But that is to misunderstand apocalyptic imagery. We have already met the idea of an individual representing and embodying an entire nation: 'You are that head of gold', said of Nebuchadnezzar in 2:38, as indeed the individual beasts represent nations.

Moreover, this figure represents not only restored Israel but the whole of redeemed humanity. So it is that in Chapter 2 of his letter, the author of *Hebrews* sees the son of man in Psalm 8 as fulfilled in Jesus 'crowned with glory and honour' and 'bringing many sons to glory' (Heb. 2:9-10). This is humankind as it was created to be and realising its full maturity.

When the term 'Son of Man' is used in the Gospels of Jesus it is always on his own lips. It is interesting that the contexts in which these occur tend to be either of his suffering and death or his coming kingdom, or at times both. An example of the first is Matthew 20:18: 'The Son of Man will be betrayed ...'; of the second, Matthew 24:30: 'They will see the Son of Man coming on the clouds of the sky, with power and great glory'; of the third, Mark 14:62: 'You will see the Son of Man sitting at the right hand of the Mighty One and coming on the clouds of heaven.'

Two further striking New Testament examples are relevant at this point. In Acts 7:56, Stephen, about to face martyrdom, cries: 'Look, ... I see heaven open and the Son of Man standing at the right hand of God.' Stephen is there experiencing what Daniel 7 predicts that the beast will 'oppress' the saints who will be 'handed over to him'. Similarly, another of those saints, suffering in exile as the beast rages furiously 'was on the island of Patmos because of the word of God and the testimony of Jesus' (Rev. 1:9). There he has a vision of a glorious figure 'like a son of man' (Rev. 1:13). This is not Christ as he was, not even Christ as he will be, but Christ as he now is. This glorious reality is the controlling vision for the rest of the book of Revelation. So here, in Daniel, the vision of the throne and the Son of Man towers over the whole of human history.

Some other details of the verses invite comment. Two verbs are used of the Son of Man in verse 13: **He approached** suggests his own dignity and right to enter the court; **was led into his presence** suggests his willing submission to the one who sits on the throne. This scene is a coronation, as becomes evident in verse 14; recalling in different language the words of Psalm 2:6: 'I have installed my king on Zion, my holy hill.'

Verse 14 recalls, and is probably meant to, 3:4 where 'peoples, nations and men of every language' are commanded to worship Nebuchadnezzar's image. Indeed much of this scene alludes to earlier parts of the book and is a demonstration of its unity. Nebuchadnezzar, in forgetting that he was mortal, sank to the level of a beast (4:24ff.) and only became human again when he acknowledged that there was only one King who reigned in his own right and whose kingdom was eternal. Moreover, in Chapter 6, the normally raging beasts have been rendered impotent. The future belongs not to them, nor to the ancient powers of chaos, but to one 'like a son of man', one with God who is also one of us:

> Crown him the Son of God,
> Before the worlds began;
> And ye who tread where he has trod,
> Crown him the Son of Man.[9]

---

[9] From the hymn 'Crown him with many crowns' by M. Bridges and G. Thring.

The Interpretation (7:15-27)

We have already noticed in Chapter 2 that vision is the raw material of revelation and that interpretation is necessary. These next verses give an interpretation of the visions and concentrate on the fourth beast. But we begin with the effect on Daniel (see also v. 28).

> ¹⁵'I, Daniel, was troubled in spirit, and the visions that passed through my mind disturbed me.'

It is not easy or amusing to receive visions and revelation. Ezekiel, in similar circumstances, is 'overwhelmed' (Ezek. 3:15), and Jeremiah speaks of 'anguish' and 'agony of heart' (Jer. 4:19). In the book itself when Nebuchadnezzar had his dream of the same realities 'his mind was troubled and he could not sleep' (2:1). The fact that the end is certain does not remove the need for faith and courage on the journey.

> ¹⁶'I approached one of those standing there and asked him the true meaning of all this.
> So he told me and gave me the interpretation of these things.'

One of those standing there (lit. 'the standing ones') is a semi-technical term for members of the heavenly court and is in keeping with the common Old Testament idea that prophetic revelation is received in that court. Thus in 1 Kings 17:1, Elijah's statement: 'The LORD, the God of Israel ... before whom I stand' (NKJV) is an assertion that he has stood in the court of heaven and heard the message there. This idea is developed further here in Daniel where both in this and later chapters angel interpreters expound the meaning of events. Similarly in Ezekiel 40-48 an angel guide unfolds the new city and temple, as does the angel in Revelation 21:9. Thus what we have here is not Daniel's reflections on the vision, it is an authoritative interpretation.

> ¹⁷'The four great beasts are four kingdoms that will rise from the earth. ¹⁸But the saints of the Most High will receive the kingdom and will possess it for ever – yes, for ever and ever.'

It is worth noting that here the beasts rise from the earth rather than the sea. This is not a contradiction but rather a reminder that in Apocalyptic different images are used to express the same reality. We already saw the many-layered nuances of the 'great sea', and here the reference is probably to the nations, who in Isaiah 17:13 roar like the raging waves. Similarly in Revelation 13 there are two beasts, one rising from the sea and one from the earth.

This interplay of images helps in the understanding of the next detail in verse 18. The kingdom is to be received by **the saints of the Most High** who have not been mentioned in the original vision. Obviously the meaning given to the saints, **'holy ones'**, is related to the identity of the 'Son of Man'. In our discussion of that phrase we noticed how this figure is both related to God and to humanity and that his triumph also involves the triumph of those whom he represents. In Revelation 17 the woman and the beast, who is also the persecuting power of economic and military totalitarianism, make war on the Lamb but fails 'because he is Lord of lords and King of kings'. But also associated with him in his victory are 'his chosen and faithful followers'. It is interesting to see how here in verses 23-25 the terms 'king' and 'kingdom' are used interchangeably with the head often standing for all the people.

The 'holy ones' are referred to in 4:17 where they are clearly angels, and in Hebrew this is its common meaning, for example, Psalm 89:6 and Job 5:1. However, in Psalm 34:9 the term clearly applies to human beings. In Leviticus 19:2 the adjective is used: 'Be holy because I, the LORD your God, am holy', and by inter-testamental literature, the word could be used both of heavenly and earthly beings. This link of saints and angels is underlined in a great passage in Hebrews 12 where the author sees the same reality as Daniel does here:

But you have come to Mount Zion ... to thousands upon thousands of angels in joyful assembly, to the church of the firstborn whose names are written in heaven (Heb. 12:22ff.).

Thus the reality of the heavenly court is complex and cannot be collapsed into one image.

The title used here of God, **'the Most High'**, is plural, as it is in verses 22, 25 and 27, and probably is the so-called 'plural of majesty'. Its use here marginalises all alternative centres of power, supernatural or human, and in a sense encapsulates the theology of the chapter.

Daniel shows true human qualities here. He is not in doubt about the final outcome but naturally quails at the rough road to be travelled before it is reached. He is also deeply concerned at the savage persecution the saints will have to endure under the rampaging activities of the fourth beast.

> [19]'Then I wanted to know the true meaning of the fourth beast, which was different from all the others and most terrifying, with its iron teeth and bronze claws – the beast that crushed and devoured its victims and trampled underfoot whatever was left. [20]I also wanted to know about the ten horns on its head and about the other horn that came up, before which three of them fell – the horn that looked more imposing than the others and that had eyes and a mouth that spoke boastfully. [21]As I watched, this horn was waging war against the saints and defeating them, [22]until the Ancient of Days came and pronounced judgment in favour of the saints of the Most High, and the time came when they possessed the kingdom.'

The vision goes on even as Daniel is asking questions – **as I watched** (v. 21). These verses concentrate on the deadly power of the fourth beast, with the added detail that it has bronze claws. A detail in verse 21 that **the horn was waging war against the saints** is important. This warfare, as we shall learn in Chapter 10, is both heavenly and earthly and indeed the outcome of the earthly battle depends on the result of the heavenly one.

And so to the interpretation:

> [23]'He gave me this explanation: "The fourth beast is a fourth kingdom that will appear on earth. It will be different from all the other kingdoms and will devour the whole earth, trampling it down

and crushing it. [24]The ten horns are ten kings who will come from this kingdom. After them another king will arise, different from the earlier ones; he will subdue three kings. [25]He will speak against the Most High and oppress his saints and try to change the set times and the laws. The saints will be handed over to him for a time, times and half a time.

[26]'But the court will sit, and his power will be taken away and completely destroyed for ever. [27]Then the sovereignty, power and greatness of the kingdoms under the whole heaven will be handed over to the saints, the people of the Most High. His kingdom will be an everlasting kingdom, and all rulers will worship and obey him.'

The repetition of various themes and motifs in these verses, a literary technique we have already met, especially in Chapter 3, helps to fix clearly the main actors on the stage and the main issues at stake. It would be useful to remind ourselves of a principle of interpretation already noted in the discussion of verse 12. The view of history here springs from, but is not confined to, the time of the seer nor the centuries immediately following. The four kingdoms of Babylon, Persia, Greece and Rome do arise successively and play their part in the actual history of the ancient world. More specifically, the tyranny of Antiochus Epiphanes is to become the focus of the next four chapters. Yet these events do not exhaust the meaning of the vision which also reveals the inner nature of human power of which these régimes were simply examples. Thus if the sequence sometimes seems linear, and at other times to speak of parallel régimes, we should not be surprised because both levels of meaning are true.

The activities of the beast are universal in their scope and totally destructive. Here we are seeing the general power of military and economic totalitarianism throughout the centuries. If the little horn is Antiochus, then we have clearly not to expect linear historical sequence here because the ten kings could not then arise from Rome. More probably what is happening is that the ten horns represent the whole of human history and that the little horn, manifested partially in Antiochus, is fully seen at the

End in the final antichrist, the man of sin.

More significant is the nature of the régime established by 'the little horn' or the eleventh king. First there is blasphemy: **He will speak against the Most High** (v. 25). Then there is persecution: **he will oppress the saints**. Then there is the attempt to change the whole pattern of life: **try to change the set times and the laws**. This would involve revision of the calendar and suppression of Israel's holy days, as well as virtually taking history into his own hands and making himself a god. At first all this seems to succeed: **The saints will be handed over to him**.

Yet once again the limitations of his power are decreed; this will last only **for a time, times and half a time**. Antiochus desecrated the temple in 167 BC and after Judas Maccabaeus' victories it was rededicated it in 164. Thus we have a period of approximately three and a half years. The important point here is not to insist on precise dates nor on the identification of the little horn with Antiochus, but rather to see this time as a particular illustration of the godless power which oppresses the saints throughout history, yet whose power is limited to a specific period decreed by the Most High. An additional nuance could be that the entire period is not one of persecution, there are times when it ceases even before the End comes.

Verses 26 and 27 take us out of any immediate historical settings to the ultimate truth and the final outcome of history. The rise and fall of the ten kingdoms were judgments within history, this is the judgment *on* history. Thus while the court always sits this is the last great assize.

> When at the world's last session,
> The dreadful Judge in middle air shall spread his throne.[10]

Exactly how all this fits into the pattern of events outlined in Revelation 19–22 is far from clear. Does this refer to an earthly reign of Christ and his saints during the Millennium as at least one reading of Revelation 20:4 would suggest? Or does it simply

---

[10] 'Ode on the Morning of Christ's Nativity' by John Milton.

refer to the final triumph of the Kingdom of God without any specific time reference? Discussion of these issues go far beyond the scope of this commentary, but two things at least can be said.

The first is that this kingdom is no mere metaphor or mythical symbol saying little more than that things will get better and the future is bright. This kingdom is established tangibly and literally in the same way as the other régimes are actual powers which appear on the world stage. The symbols used demonstrate the actuality of these events. This is not simply happening in some imaginative landscape of the mind, rather we are being given an insight into the realities behind the events of history. The coming kingdom is more, not less, real than the Babylonian empire.

The second is that the explanation of history is not to be found in history itself. It is from outside that the answer will come. Yet the figure who comes from outside is humanlike as well as one with God, and thus history and creation will fulfil their purposes. The judgments of God stretch throughout all history and work through secondary causes such as historians can examine. These causes, such as economic decline, political instability, inspirational leaders and so on, are not insignificant in themselves, they are not however, the ultimate causes. However, the great saving events of the cross, resurrection and ascension set in motion 'the last days' which will culminate in the final coming of the kingdom which will last for ever.

The Effect on Daniel (7:28)

> 'This is the end of the matter. I, Daniel, was deeply troubled by my thoughts, and my face turned pale, but I kept the matter to myself.'

Matter is literally 'word' and confirms the emphasis that the whole vision, including the interpretation, has been a revelation from God. As in verse 15 the cost and painfulness of receiving such revelation is underlined. **I kept the matter to myself** shows Daniel's concern that there was much here to meditate on and much that was still unclear.

Here we come to the end of the Aramaic section of the book, the text now reverting to Hebrew. It may well be that the Aramaic part of the book was circulated separately to reach a wider audience with the essence of the book's message, but this cannot be proved.

General Comments

This is a magnificent chapter sweeping through all time and space and written in a powerful and imaginative style. Yet it is not free-standing and, as we have seen, it is linked closely with the stories of Chapters 1–6. As we shall see, Chapters 8–12 develop, in different ways, themes which are given panoramic treatment in Chapter 7. Five comments will help to bring together some of the main implications of this chapter.

1. This chapter helpfully illustrates the relationship between faith and knowledge. As we have seen, there are some schools of thought which turn such a chapter into a detailed blueprint of future events, confidently identifying the ten kings and the little horn and the exact spheres of their activities. On the other hand, some dissolve this into a vague dream of an idealistic future. The point, it seems to me, is that there are a number of certainties: the throne of God, the rise and fall of human power, the intervention of the Son of Man, the inevitability of persecution and suffering, and the final triumph of the Kingdom of God. These are facts and not simply ideas, and are worked out in history on the international, national, communal and personal levels. We must not fall into the error of assuming that because we cannot say everything we cannot say anything. Yet faith is needed. Often the beast appears to triumph, for we can see him clearly, yet the throne of God and the coming of the Son of Man are invisible. It is only these assurances which will help us to

stand when victory seems a remote and even impossible reality. 'This is the victory that has overcome the world, even our faith' (1 John 5:4). Certainty about the final outcome does not make faith invalid; indeed faith is the more necessary when so often the actual events seem to mock the reality of such an outcome.

2. The chapter also illustrates the relationship between divine sovereignty and free will. It is often argued that predictive prophecy makes human beings puppets whose destinies are already determined. Nothing here suggests such a mechanical and deterministic view of human history. It is indeed true that the beasts are 'given' their authority, yet in their time they have considerable freedom to act and plan. It is just here that the mysterious interplay of God's sovereignty and human responsibility lies and nowhere is this better illustrated than in the stories of Nebuchadnezzar and Belshazzar which form the background to this chapter. Both of them receive the same opportunities and responsibilities, yet both react very differently. The Babylonian empire, the head of gold and the lion with eagle's wings, does indeed fall as predicted; yet there is no doubt that Belshazzar's blasphemous irresponsibility had no small part to play in this, as Daniel makes clear in 5:22-24. Another example of a different kind is seen in Chapter 9 where the end of Exile is decreed, but the prayers of God's people play a part in that event. God's purposes are indeed fulfilled, but at every stage, humans are given choices and these choices are real.

3. This chapter is a further depiction of the nature of power which we have already seen dramatised in the stories of Chapters 1–6. God's power and God's representative is heavenly; human power rises from the sea and earth. The beast is destroyed by the fire which represents the blazing holiness of God. As we have seen, the chapter is fair in its assessment of human power and the first three beasts are a mixture of good and bad. However, as Chapters 1–6 make plain, human power is only strong when it recognises its derivative nature. Nebuchadnezzar did. Belshazzar did

not. Similarly, the power exercised by Daniel (and his three friends) has been that of faith and integrity. Thus, as we have seen, in the stories of Chapters 1–6, the life of the world to come has been partially anticipated, not only in the miraculous events of Chapters 3 and 6, but in the godly lives of Daniel and his friends.

4. This chapter throws a great deal of light on the nature of revelation. Visions, pictures and symbols remain confusing until an authoritative word is spoken. Much mystery remains but there is enough light given to make possible godly living in the world. The blend of vision and interpretation in the chapter helps us to avoid two apposite errors.

One is to make this and similar chapters in Apocalyptic literature into detailed blueprints of the future and attempt to identify exactly who the ten kings are and how long they reign. This kind of interpretation often robs the passage of present application and reduces the study of Apocalyptic to a kind of riddle-solving which is satisfied when people and places can be identified.

The second is to detach the chapter from history and make it simply a dream-like medley dramatising the age-long struggle of good and evil. But the chapter will not allow us to do this. The symbols suggest the solid reality of the kingdoms which appear in historical time and in real places. Similarly the coming of the Son of Man is not just a poetic way of saying good will triumph but an actual event. And it is just here that the whole crux of revelation is to be found.

'And beginning with Moses and all the Prophets, he explained to them what was said in all the Scriptures concerning himself' (Luke 24:27). With the coming of Christ we are in the 'last days' which will culminate with his coming again in glory. It is the great saving events of the birth, death, resurrection, ascension, coming and future glory of Christ which open this chapter to our understanding. Thus by faith 'we see Jesus ... crowned with glory and honour' (Heb. 2:9). So this chapter becomes 'a light shining in a dark place, until the day dawns and the morning star rises in your hearts' (2 Pet. 1:19).

5. The close links of this chapter with Chapters 1–6 as well as the precise dating of its visions are important. In Chapters 1–6 the author has concentrated on a number of apparently disconnected stories of a small number of Jewish exiles. Here in Chapter 7 we have set out what was often implied in earlier chapters, that is, how these stories fit into the great story, the Bible's plot line which is the narrative of God's purposes from creation to consummation. Just as in *Job*, the story moves on two levels: the human events on earth and the greater reality of how these events are orchestrated in the court of heaven. These are ultimately linked by the 'Son of Man' who comes from heaven and takes humanity. But these realities are only to be perceived by faith. Faith does not mean optimism or taking a positive view of world events. Faith is hearing the word of revelation and obeying it so that in the actual circumstances of this world we can live in the contemporary in the light of the eternal.

Questions for further study

1. How does Apocalyptic literature help us to live in the present?

2. 'Beginning with Moses and all the prophets, he explained to them what was said in all the Scriptures concerning himself' (Luke 24:27). What does this chapter tell us about Christ?

3. What is the nature of human power according to this chapter?

8

Your will be done

We turn now from a panoramic sweep of human history to concentrate on a limited period, the overthrow of Persia and the rise of Greece. The vision is clearly linked with those in Chapter 7 and this chapter, indeed the rest of the book, can be seen as a development of some of the ideas and issues raised in that chapter. We shall examine, more briefly here, and in more detail in Chapter 11, why there is such concentration on this period and how this fits in with the overall theology of the book.

The Setting (8:1-2)
Characteristically we begin with a note of time and place, here given with a fair amount of detail.

> [1]In the third year of King Belshazzar's reign, I, Daniel, had a vision, after the one that had already appeared to me. [2]In my vision I saw myself in the citadel of Susa in the province of Elam; in the vision I was beside the Ulai canal.

The significance of receiving both visions in the time of Belshazzar is fairly clear. In Chapter 5 it was noted that Daniel had obviously been marginalised at Belshazzar's court. However, he is far from marginalised by God, and the magnificent sweep of Chapter 7 and the more specific focus of this chapter gives Daniel an unparalleled insight into the ways of God in history and enables him to stand firm. Belshazzar's time is running out, but the end is not yet, and there is very much more to happen and even tougher and more testing times ahead before the Kingdom comes.

The third year of Belshazzar would be 550/549 BC. Baldwin[1]

---

[1] Baldwin, p. 155.

points out that this was the year when Cyrus supplanted the Median leader Astyages and welded Media/Persia together, with Persia becoming the dominant partner. The activities of Cyrus match exactly the growing power of the ram in the vision. Elam was to the north of the Persian Gulf, roughly between Babylon and Persia. Susa, the 'citadel' or 'capital' (occurring regularly in the book of Esther), was seen as the heart of the Persian empire and is thus a most appropriate place for this vision to unfold. Ulai was one of the waterways near the city. On its banks, just as Ezekiel had his vision by the Kebar Canal, so Daniel has this revelation.

The Vision (8:3-14)
Initially, at least, the vision is relatively straightforward, with the two animals being identified in verses 20-21. However, there are many difficulties and obscurities in the detail. But, to the vision itself.

> [3]I looked up, and there before me was a ram with two horns, standing bedside the canal, and the horns were long. One of the horns was longer than the other but grew up later. [4]I watched the ram as he charged towards the west and the north and the south. No animal could stand against him, and none could rescue from his power. He did as he pleased and became great.

Ezekiel 34:17 mentions rams and goats together as symbols of power. The two horns represent Media and Persia, with the now dominant Persia as the longer of the two. Verse 4 probably describes the rapid conquests of Cyrus as he pushed into Babylonia and Asia Minor. In Isaiah 41:2 he is described as 'one from the east', accounting for the omission of that direction here. He **became great**, more exactly 'he did great things', is often used of God himself (for example, 1 Sam. 12:24 and Ps. 126:2-3). However, when used of humans it tends to suggest overweening arrogance; for example, of mockers in Psalm 35:26 and of enemies in Psalm 55:12. The final manifestation of this attitude is found in Revelation 13:4: 'who is like the beast? Who can make war against him?'

Yet just at its moment of overweening power, the ram is totally destroyed by a new opponent:

> [5]As I was thinking about this, suddenly a goat with a prominent horn between his eyes came from the west, crossing the whole earth without touching the ground. [6]He came towards the two-horned ram I had seen standing beside the canal and charged at him in great rage. [7]I saw him attack the ram furiously, striking the ram and shattering his two horns. The ram was powerless to stand against him; the goat knocked him to the ground and trampled on him, and none could rescue the ram from his power. [8]The goat became very great, but at the height of his power his large horn was broken off, and in its place four prominent horns grew up towards the four winds of heaven.'

Crossing the whole earth without touching the ground obviously refers to the spectacularly swift conquests of Alexander the Great. In 334 BC, at the Granicus River, he won a dashing and incredibly risky victory over a Persian army holding a strong position. In the following year, facing Darius III of Persia on the battlefield at Issus, by brilliant cavalry tactics he won another victory. In 331, a yet more decisive victory was won at Gaugemela; all this while he was still in his early twenties. Verse 7 gives us a vivid impression of that amazing conquest which has few parallels in world history.

Yet, mighty as he was, Alexander's career was cut short, and he died in Babylon at the age of thirty-two. His death was surrounded by portents, omens and dark rumours of poison. His empire collapsed almost immediately (**his large horn was broken off**) and he was succeeded by his four generals: Ptolemy Lagus, Philip Aridacus, Antigonus and Seleucus Nicanor. It is the fourth of these, the Seleucid Empire in Syria, which is now our concern.

Before leaving the vision of the ram and the he-goat a comment on style is in order. This is one of the most vivid pictures in the book marked by great clarity and a sense of movement. There is also an appeal to the ear as well as to the eye. We can almost hear the crash of the animals as they battle it out and the splintering sound of the horns. By such means the author draws us into his vision.

Yet this vision is only the backdrop for a subsequent conflict which is not to be between two earthly powers, but between a human and God himself.

> [9]Out of one of them came another horn which started small but grew in power to the south and to the east and towards the Beautiful Land. [10]It grew until it reached the host of the heavens, and it threw some of the starry host down to the earth and trampled on them. [11]It set itself up to be as great as the Prince of the host; it took away the daily sacrifice from him, and the place of his sanctuary was brought low. [12]Because of rebellion, the host (of the saints) and the daily sacrifice were given over to it. It prospered in everything it did, and truth was thrown to the ground.

The growing horn, who is Antiochus IV,[2] from one perspective is quite insignificant but, as these verses make clear, from the standpoint of the Divine overview of history his activities, like those of the fourth beast, express a peculiar evil. Moreover, the object of his attack is the **Beautiful Land**. This expression is also used in Ezekiel 20:6 and 15 where it is also called the 'land flowing with milk and honey'. Thus the advance of Antiochus effectively threatens another Exile, this one yet more deadly because he wants to set up idolatry in the very heart of Israel's faith.

The supernatural nature of this conflict is brought out clearly in verse 10 with the little horn's attack on the heavenly host. The heavenly hosts mean both members of the heavenly court and the stars. Later the idea is developed of angels being associated with particular heavenly bodies. But the link is clear throughout the Old Testament. In Deuteronomy 17:3 they are linked in a stern warning against idolatry. In Job 38:7 God lays

---

2 See Introduction, p. 13 for historical sketch.

the foundations of the earth and 'the morning stars sang together and all the angels shouted for joy'. Also in Isaiah 14:13 the King of Babylon wants to raise his throne 'above the stars of God'. All this indicates a more sinister power behind Antiochus and we shall see in Chapter 10 the influence of angel powers on earthly conflicts.

The Prince of the host (v. 11) is therefore probably not the high priest but God himself whose temple is under attack. The daily sacrifice (see Exod. 29:38-42 and Num. 28:2-8) consisted of a lamb with a libation of flour and wine, but here may refer to the whole range of sacrifices which Antiochus suppressed. Moreover, the **bringing low** of the sanctuary shows the seriousness of what is happening. During the Exile the temple was literally destroyed, but here 'Babylon' usurps the temple with its own worship and usurps the true God and his worship. 1 Maccabees 1 tells us of how Antiochus stole the Temple treasures (1:20-24); forbade Jewish worship (1:44ff) and, worst of all, built a pagan altar over the altar of burnt offering (1:54ff.). A crisis of as great a magnitude as the Exile is envisaged.

Verse 12 is obscure in detail, although the general sense is clear enough. The **rebellion** (also in v. 13) is almost certainly the blasphemous arrogance of Antiochus. The NIV interprets **host** by following it with **the saints** in brackets, the phrase literally reads 'the host was given over to it', 'it' presumably being the little horn. This does not mean that the host cannot be the heavenly host as suggested earlier. Rather the attacks of Antiochus on God's people reflect the heavenly conflict. Also given over to it was the daily sacrifice, which may refer to the setting up of the pagan altar already mentioned. **Truth was thrown to the ground** probably refers initially to the destruction of Torah scrolls by Antiochus. This concentration on the importance of the Word of God carries on in Chapter 9.

The link of heavenly and earthly involvement in these events is underlined in the next two verses where two **holy ones**, members of the heavenly court, speak about the desecration of the sanctuary.

> ¹³Then I heard a holy one speaking, and another holy one said to
> him, 'How long will it take for the vision to be fulfilled – the
> vision concerning the daily sacrifice, the rebellion that causes deso-
> lation, and the surrender of the sanctuary and of the host that will
> be trampled underfoot?'
>   ¹⁴He said to me, 'It will take 2,300 evenings and mornings;
> then the sanctuary will be reconsecrated.'

Two important factors emerge from these verses. The first is
that the course of history is not fully comprehensible by the
heavenly court. The second is the question 'how long'? which
is not questioning the rightness of God's ways but suffering along
with the oppressed people, and, as in many of the Lament psalms,
mourning for the desolation of the city and temple. A good
example of this is Psalm 74:10: 'How long will the enemy mock
you, O God?' The cry is for God to limit the time of evil.

The rebellion that causes desolation, also **the abomination that causes desolation** (9:27, 11:31 and 12:11), may have
as its primary meaning the pagan altar but plainly the entire
activity of Antiochus is in view. The **trampling underfoot** picks
up a detail from the goat's furious attack on the ram (v. 7) and
reminds us of the unity of the whole vision.

The question 'how long?' receives a specific answer: **It will
take 2,300 evenings and mornings.** This is usually taken to
mean the occasions on which the daily sacrifices were offered:
i.e., 1,150 days. This is rather less than 'the time, times and half
a time' (7:25) in which the saints are handed over. However, it
seems reasonable to see it as the same approximate period when
Antiochus desecrated the Temple. Antiochus desecrated the
Temple in 167 BC, and following the decisive victory by Judas
Maccabaeus the temple was reconsecrated in 164. This period
of roughly three and a half years becomes in apocalyptic literature
not just the literal period of Antiochus but a symbol of that
prolonged but limited period when God's people are subjected
to the power of the beast. Thus in Revelation 12, the woman is
attacked by the dragon for a period variously described as 1,260
days (v. 6) or 'a time, times and half a time' (v. 14). However,

as becomes clear in later verses, the reconsecrating of the temple is far more than the events of 164.

The Interpretation (8:15:26)

It is not clear if Daniel is still involved in the vision or reflecting on it, but in any case this time he does not need to ask for an interpretation (cf. 7:15).

> [15]While I, Daniel was watching the vision and trying to understand it, there before me stood one who looked like a man. [16]And I heard a man's voice from the Ulai calling, 'Gabriel, tell this man the meaning of the vision.'
> [17]As he came near the place where I was standing, I was terrified and fell prostrate. 'Son of man,' he said to me, "understand" that the vision concerns the time of the end.'
> [18]While he was speaking to me, I was in a deep sleep with my face to the ground. Then he touched me and raised me to my feet.

Just as in Chapter 7, God's power is different from that of the animals, so here the revelation from heaven is spoken in a human voice. The agent of the revelation is Gabriel who is described as **one who looked like a man**. The word used here, *geber*, means particularly a strong man, but not in a swaggering sense, rather because of his relationship to God. Gabriel and Michael are the only named angels in Scripture, but in 1 Enoch we also meet such angels as Raphael and Uriel. However, Gabriel is not himself the originator of the revelation. The **man's voice** (v. 16) is that of God himself, and when Gabriel speaks to Daniel, the form of address he uses to him is **Son of man**, the characteristic way in which God addresses Ezekiel, another of the links of this chapter with that book.

Daniel is terrified and falls on his face, overwhelmed by a deep sleep. This kind of experience is referred to elsewhere. In Genesis 15:12 Abraham falls into a deep sleep and is overwhelmed by darkness as he hears rather similar news: his people are to be terribly oppressed but will be delivered. This vision, says Gabriel, **concerns the time of the end**.

'The end' is the key to understanding this vision. It refers first to the end of the specific events here, that prolonged but limited period. No human power or earthly situation lasts for ever. Yet, at the same time, these events foreshadow the End of all things, just as all the great crises of history reflect something of the reality of the End. Indeed this is made explicit in the next verse.

> [19]He said: 'I am going to tell you what will happen later in the time of wrath, because the vision concerns the appointed time of the end.'

The wrath of God falls on those who rebel against him. His own people had cause to know this, for the Exile itself was such a time, and Zechariah 1:12 refers specifically to this. Thus, while what follows refers to Persia and Greece, and in particular to Antiochus, these régimes are simply manifestations of the devilish power which continually opposes the coming of the Kingdom of God.

> [20]'The two-horned ram that you saw represents the kings of Media and Persia. [21]The shaggy goat is the king of Greece, and the large horn between his eyes is the first king. [22]The four horns that replaced the one that was broken off represent four kingdoms that will emerge from his nation but will not have the same power.'

The interpretation of the vision is clear and precise. It is an important reminder not to be pedantic in the understanding of the details. Thus the goat is the Great Empire but more specifically Alexander who is also the horn. The animals are both kings and kingdoms. This is also an interesting sidelight on the use of the word **king**. As we noticed in Chapter 5, some scholars object to the words 'king', 'kingdom' and the like being used in relation to Belshazzar. But this chapter shows that the word 'king' is used of the régime in power whether the individual at the head of it was called 'king' or not. But here, the kingdom which is particularly significant is the Seleucid kingdom out of which arises Antiochus.

Here the apocalyptic language is replaced by a swift character sketch:

> [23]'In the latter part of their reign, when rebels have become com-
> pletely wicked, a stern-faced king, a master of intrigue, will arise.
> [24]He will become very strong, but not by his own power. He will
> cause astounding devastation and will succeed in whatever he does.
> He will destroy the mighty men and the holy people. [25]He will
> cause deceit to prosper, and he will consider himself superior. When
> they feel secure, he will destroy many and take his stand against
> the Prince of princes. Yet he will be destroyed, but not by human
> power.'

God allows the sins of these kingdoms to become extreme before
he intervenes with radical judgment. Similarly in Genesis 15:16
God postpones judgment 'for the sin of the Amorites has not
yet reached the full measure'. This is another example of how
both God's purposes work out unfailingly and yet humans have
responsibility for their attitudes and actions. This is indeed being
worked out in Daniel's own setting in the behaviour of
Belshazzar.

Out of and embodying this general rebelliousness which is
to characterise the closing years of what was once Alexander's
empire, **a stern-faced king will arise**. The phrase translated
'stern-faced' is the same as that used of the adulteress in Proverbs
7:13. There, the dark lady of Chapter 7 is contrasted with wisdom
of Chapter 8. Here, combined with the statement that he is **a
master of intrigue**, there is probably another reflection on the
nature of power. The phrase 'master of intrigue' or its Aramaic
equivalent is used in a positive sense of Daniel in 5:12. Antiochus
is the opposite of the wise who, as Chapter 12:3 tells us, 'will
shine like the brightness of the heavens'. This ruler has enormous
power because of his diplomatic abilities. 2 Maccabees 4:7-29
outlines his success in manipulating the high priestly circles.

The phrase in verse 24, **not by his own power**[3], is a fascinat-

---

[3] Some commentators argue that the phrase in verse 24 – 'not by his own
power' – is a gloss, but this is unsupported by manuscript evidence.

ing one. We must remember the whole sweep of Chapters 7 and 8 and the picture of real human régimes which nevertheless are only manifestations of demonic forces which engage in a titanic struggle with God. Thus the meaning of this passage is not exhausted by Antiochus; rather it points to the final Antichrist who will appear in the final days and embody the evil features of all the many antichrists who have already been (see 1 John 2:18).

Antiochus indulged in great cruelty; killing many thousands as well as profaning the temple and making extensive use of a network of spies and traitors. All this culminates in his supreme blasphemy as he **takes his stand against the Prince of princes**. By attacking God's people and his sanctuary he is attacking God himself. This will result in the destruction of Antiochus, **but not by human power**. Antiochus in fact died sometime in November/December 164. The circumstances of his death from a painful disease while returning from Persia were mysterious. 1 Maccabees 6:9 speaks of a 'deep grief which continually gripped him'; 2 Maccabees 9 speaks of an agonising internal pain and the 'end of his life by a most pitiable fate, among the mountains in a strange land'. We have a striking parallel in the death of Herod in Acts 12:23.

The reliability of the vision and its interpretation is now underlined.

[26]'The vision of the evenings and mornings that has been given you is true, but seal up the vision, for it concerns the distant future.'

This assurance of the reliability of revelation is also given in 10:1 and 11:2 and is also a feature of the end of the book of Revelation itself (see 19:9; 21:5; 22:6). **Seal up the vision** does not mean that Apocalyptic was an esoteric kind of truth for an initiated élite. Rather it suggests that it has particular relevance to a time yet future. In Daniel's own time, nearly four centuries were to pass before the time of Antiochus, and since that time did not exhaust the meaning of the vision its complete fulfilment remains in the future. Yet for Christian readers, the End is already upon us. We live in the 'last days' because the Son of Man has come and given the death blow to every Antiochus. But we still await his final triumph. I shall say more of this in the general comments.

The Effect on Daniel (8:27)

Any idea that the truth of this chapter is irrelevant to ordinary living because 'it concerns the distant future' is dispelled by the final verse:

> I, Daniel, was exhausted and lay ill for several days. Then I got up and went about the king's business. I was appalled by the vision; it was beyond understanding.

Daniel, as in Chapter 7 (and in 4:19), finds this revelation overwhelming and exhausting. Seeing into the Divine councils involves sharing something of the Divine sorrow at human wickedness and the compassion for the suffering of his people. The word **appalled** or *desolated* is the same as the word used for the abominable desolation in 8:13; 9:27 and 12:11. Daniel has seen something of evil as God sees it and thus cannot be complacent or indifferent.

Yet very far from neglecting his daily work he **went about the king's business**. Under Belshazzar that was much more lowly and probably more tedious than the status he had know under Nebuchadnezzar and would know again under the Persian empire.

One further detail is worth noting. Daniel says the vision **was beyond understanding**. This does not mean he did not understand it at all, but that the full significance was hidden to him. That full understanding belongs to God himself; he does, however, give us enough understanding to live effectively for him in this world.

General Comments

Chapters 7 and 8 have given us a unique glimpse into the realities behind history. Chapter 7 on a panoramic scale and Chapter 8 by focusing on a particular period in which these realities are evidenced particularly vividly. Four observations will help us to sum up our study of both chapters and Chapter 8 in particular.

1. This chapter gives us a clear insight into the nature of predictive prophecy. Many commentators dismiss this, but give no reason other than disbelief that God can reveal himself in this way.[4] Part of the supremacy of the God of Israel lies in this, that he can foresee the future because he is the Lord of history. But, as already commented, this does not reduce humans to robots nor removes their responsibility. Indeed what God does here is an illustration of Amos 3:7: 'Surely the Sovereign LORD does nothing without revealing his plan to his servants, the prophets.'

I believe the key to understanding predictive passages in prophecy and Apocalyptic is above all to relate them to Christ. We do not have a detailed blueprint of the future, the account is selective and, while it refers to the age of Antiochus, it goes far beyond it to find its full meaning in the last days and the conflict between the Beast and the Son of Man. This gives the book a permanent relevance and shows its importance in the Bible's story line.

2. This also helps to explain the concentration on the age of Antiochus. He, like the King of Babylon in Isaiah 14, wants to storm the throne of God. Like Pharaoh in a much earlier age he will recognise no authority but his own. Daniel is being shown

---

[4] W. Sibley Towner in his commentary on *Daniel* (John Knox Press, Atlanta 1984) writes: 'Human beings are unable accurately to predict future events centuries in advance and to say that Daniel could do so, even on the basis of a symbolic revelation vouchsafed to him by God and interpreted by an angel, is to fly in the face of the certainties of human nature' (p. 115). This is to set human reason above divine revelation.

that this kind of blasphemous arrogance is not exhausted by any one régime but will appear again and again. This makes it necessary to prepare God's people to be ready for it. Once again the two parts of the book hang together for it is the sacrilege of Belshazzar in using the Temple vessels in Chapter 5 which is closely parallel to Antiochus' blasphemous behaviour here. Antiochus is the embodiment of that godless power which in all ages opposes God's kingdom.

3. Chapter 8 is a very practical demonstration of the effect that prophecy has on God's servants. He does not doubt that in the end God will triumph, but he is distressed at the thought of the suffering to be gone through before that happens. This is a caution to us when we too readily assume that we will see the cause of the gospel triumph in our time. It is, of course, always right to pray for this and to work faithfully for it. But God gives no guarantees that he will bring about a revival at any particular time. This is not always taken sufficiently seriously by those who tell us to 'claim' particular areas or times by faith. God will work in his time, not ours. It may be that he will bring a revival in our day but whether he does or not we must continue faithfully with the task he has given us.

4. Closely connected to this is that God gives us a word to live by. We have already seen the importance of how the vision is explained by the word. This links directly with Chapter 9 where we shall explore the importance of the earlier prophetic words for Daniel himself. Verse 26 with its message of 'sealing up' the vision for the distant future is also important. The word we are given is not only for us, it is given to pass on and use for the benefit of generations yet to come. Meanwhile, in the confidence that the Lord reigns we can go about whatever task God calls us to.

Questions for further study

1. What does this chapter tell us about genuine vision?

2. What is the relationship between revelation and working things out? (see especially verses 15ff.).

3. 'The time of the end'. What does this say about the interpretation of this chapter?

9

The prayer of faith

'More things are wrought by prayer than this world dreams of,' wrote Tennyson.[1] Yet the relationship of prayer to the purposes of God and how far it is a factor in the achieving of those purposes remains an area of mystery. We have already seen, in the discussion particularly of Chapter 7, how the fulfilment of God's plans does not override human responsibility; and in this chapter we will explore how the prayers of God's people are a vital part of those plans.

This chapter, and indeed the rest of the book, is set in the Persian period but looks well beyond that.

The Setting (9:1-3)

[1]In the first year of Darius, son of Xerxes (a Mede by descent), who was made ruler over the Babylonian kingdom – [2]in the first year of his reign, I, Daniel, understood from the Scriptures, according to the word of the LORD given to Jeremiah the prophet, that the desolation of Jerusalem would last seventy years.

This chapter is set in the first year of the Persian empire and is thus parallel to the events of the lions' den in Chapter 6. The year is 539 BC[2], also referred to in Ezra 1:1 as a fulfilment of 'the word of the LORD spoken by Jeremiah'. What is fascinating is that the earlier visions and revelations are now underwritten and verified by an appeal to Scripture itself.

This reference to **Scriptures** or 'the books' implies a recognised canon seen as authoritative. Just as the visions have had to be interpreted, so light is to be cast on the present moment by a

---

[1] 'Morte D'Arthur' by A. Tennyson.
[2] Baldwin points out (pp. 163-164) that both 'Darius' and 'Xerxes' may be Persian throne titles (cp. Pharaoh).

reliable word. The particular Scripture is Jeremiah 25:8-14 which speaks of the nation serving the king of Babylon for seventy years. Seventy years is described in 2 Chronicles 36:21 as a time for the land to enjoy a sabbath rest which is an indication that the term has theological as well as numerical significance.[3] It reminds us of the overall control of God who 'changes times and seasons' (2:21). This is important for understanding the cryptic verses 24-27.

Some comments need to be made on the importance of Daniel's use of Scripture here. First of all, this shows the authority of Scripture. What Scripture says is what God says, and what God says happens. Moreover, as this chapter is to go on to show, that Scripture, while speaking to its own day and situation, has a much wider and always contemporary application. Scripture is not only concerned with the facts of events such as the Exile, but with its inner meaning and its place in the whole unfolding purpose of God. Thus God's dealings in the Exile cast light on what is to happen in the time of Antiochus and indeed much later.

This is another way of underlining the relevance of Scripture. We cannot live effectively for God without the continual guiding of the Word of God. Moreover, as the prayer is to demonstrate, this is not simply looking at isolated passages but a deepening understanding of the continuing story and how God's unchanging purposes are worked out in the fluctuating circumstances of human response.

Scripture when it is listened to always produces a response:

[3]So I turned to the Lord God and pleaded with him in prayer and petition, in fasting, and in sackcloth and ashes.

Here is the proof that knowing God's purposes does not lead to

---

[3] Commentators disagree over the precise beginning and ending of the period. Did it begin with the first submission of Judah to Babylon in 605 BC or with the capitulation of Jerusalem in 597 or its final fall in 587? Did it end with the first Jewish return in 538 or the completion of the temple in 517? In any case the figure of 70 is a round figure.

complacency or remove the need for believing prayer. The fact that we believe God's kingdom will come does not prevent us regularly praying, 'Your kingdom come.' This does not mean that we believe that if we neglect prayer the kingdom will not come, but it does mean that God graciously uses our prayers as part of the preparation for that coming. The intensity and discipline of Daniel's prayer is shown by the practice of fasting, and by sackcloth and ashes representing repentance. This is neither something to be dismissed nor slavishly followed. We must remember this was a private prayer and that what ultimately matters is the attitude of heart. Fasting, however, either total or partial, is certainly a feature of the prayer lives of many prayer warriors. It is not a mandatory action but nor should it be too readily set aside.

The Prayer (9:4-19)
This is one of the great prayers of the Old Testament and powerfully echoes the language of the Psalter. The keynote is to be confession. This strikingly recalls Isaiah 6. There too a vision of the glory of God has been given, and there too the prophet's response is confession: 'I am a man of unclean lips, and I live among a people of unclean lips' (Isa. 6:5).

It is also a representative as well as a deeply personal prayer. Daniel speaks on behalf of the people. He is able to do this because of the revelation God has given him and because he has seen clearly the reasons for the Exile and looks longingly for the restoration of Jerusalem. We can see here the kind of prayer which sustained him and which, of course, in Chapter 6 led him into such mortal danger.

⁴I prayed to the LORD my God and confessed:

'O Lord, the great and awesome God, who keeps his covenant of love with all who love him and obey his commands...'

These words immediately establish the basis of this prayer. The world in which Daniel lived was full of people who prayed to their gods. But this God to whom Daniel prays is Yahweh, the Lord of the Covenant, who is committed to his people by promises that he cannot and will not break. This verse goes right to the heart of what the covenant is. Because God remains faithful that covenant is not set aside in spite of the fickleness of those with whom it is made. Yet the human response is all important: **with all who love him and obey his commands**. That phrase practically sums up the essence of the covenant. It is not a contract, it is a marriage relationship. For a most poignant and beautiful expression of this, read Ezekiel 16 where the love of Yahweh for his faithless bride is embodied in the love poem. The inner meaning of Israel's history is told in this way: 'When I looked at you and saw that you were old enough for love, I spread the corner of my garment over you and covered your nakedness. I gave you my solemn oath and entered into a covenant with you, declares the Sovereign LORD and you became mine' (Ezek. 16:8).

This love goes far beyond the realm of feeling and is amplified by **obey his commands**. That is how love is expressed, that is how the relationship is sustained. This is underlined in John 14:23 where Jesus says: 'If anyone loves me, he will obey my teaching.' Without obedience love is sentimentality.

Notice how this Lord is Daniel's personal God, the Lord *my* God, and how this is balanced by the Lord *our* God (vv. 9, 13, 15). This again is at the heart of the covenant relationship. As God's people we are part of the community of faith. Yet we need an individual relationship with the Lord and it is in the interplay of the personal and the corporate that we find the reality of the covenant people of God. It is that broken relationship which Daniel now desperately longs to see restored.

⁵'We have sinned and done wrong. We have been wicked and have rebelled; we have turned away from your commands and laws. ⁶We have not listened to your servants the prophets, who spoke in your name to our kings, our princes and our fathers, and to all the people of the land.'

What is striking about these verses is their comprehensive confession of guilt. 1 John 1:9 says: 'If we confess our sins, he is faithful and just and will forgive us our sins and purify us from all unrighteousness.' The word used there for confess is *homologeo*. While realising that the etymology of words is not always a wholly reliable guide to their meaning, yet here it is very useful. John tells us to 'say the same' as God about our sins. When we confess our sin we either have a tendency to trivialise and make excuses or, on the other hand, in a kind of twisted pride paint our sins in lurid technicolour. It is also very easy to be vague. Indeed confession is often rather like going to the dentist. We hope, that as the dentist probes, he will find nothing other than the relatively minor ailment which took us there in the first place. So it is when we 'confess' our sins with bland generalisations, the Lord often says, 'Yes, but which specific sin did you have in mind?'

So here is no vague feeling of guilt. **We have sinned**; the Hebrew word *hatta'* implies going the wrong way a headlong trek away from God; **done wrong**: *'awôn* implies perversion, a lifestyle which is not pleasing to God, summed up in the English 'we have done wrong'. **We have been wicked** is the word *rasa* and implies guilt and thus deserved punishment; we **have rebelled**: *marad* is a word which implies rebellion against a legitimate sovereign. **We have turned away**: *sur* is the regular word for apostasy. Israel had been comprehensively faithless to the covenant. This could only be healed by a comprehensive turning back to God which involved a wholehearted turning back to the Word of God.

Thus they needed to return to God's **commands and laws**. The first word refers to the great principles of godly living particularly summed up in the Decalogue (Exod. 20:1-17; Deut. 5:1-21). The second word is the specific application of these principles to the situations of living. So the emphasis on the importance of Scripture continues.

It is further underlined by the phrase **your servants the prophets**, which probably here most specifically refers to Jeremiah and indeed is used in Jeremiah 26:5. It also recurs in Amos 3:7 in connection with God's revelation of his purposes. To listen to the voice of the prophets was to listen to the voice of God. This was a message for the whole of society: **our kings, our princes and fathers, and to all the people of the land**. Thus the people are without excuse. Prayer is the only way to restore that broken relationship and that prayer must be firmly rooted in Scripture.

The prayer continues with an appeal to the character of God.

> 7'Lord, you are righteous, but this day we are covered with shame – the men of Judah and people of Jerusalem and all Israel, both near and far, in all the countries where you have scattered us because of our unfaithfulness to you. 8O LORD, we and our kings, our princes and our fathers are covered with shame because we have sinned against you. 9The Lord our God is merciful and forgiving, even though we have rebelled against him; 10we have not obeyed the LORD our God or kept the laws he gave us through his servants the prophets. 11All Israel has transgressed your law and turned away, refusing to obey you.'

Daniel's confidence is not based primarily on the fact that God is merciful but that God is righteous. This is at first sight surprising because there is an almost endemic tendency in us to equate the righteousness of God exclusively with the anger of God. This was, of course, classically the experience of the young Luther and it was his discovery that only because God is righteous can he forgive. This is the great theme of the Letter to the Romans and the wellspring of all true repentance and godly living.

Essentially, the righteousness of God is his total integrity and consistency. This is what makes our repentance possible. We know exactly where we are with God. One of our failings as human beings is inconsistency. Frequently we don't know where we are with people nor they with us. But with God we know exactly what to expect. Our anger usually has a large element of injured vanity; God's anger is wholly just and consistent with his character. In particular, Daniel is appealing to God's faithfulness to his covenant with his faithless people. This is clearly expressed in Psalm 89:30-34: 'If his sons forsake my law .... I will punish their sin'; this is most obviously seen in the Exile. But then: 'I will not take my love from him, nor will I ever betray my faithfulness. I will not violate my covenant or alter what my lips have uttered.' A similar emphasis is made by John in his first Letter: '... whenever our hearts condemn us. For God is greater than our hearts and he knows everything' (1 John 3:20).

A further important point to notice is that Daniel is praying for all the people of God: **the men of Judah and people of Jerusalem and all Israel**. These include the descendants of the northern kingdom who had been deported to Assyria in that earlier exile (see 2 Kings 17). A reading of 1 and 2 Kings chronicles the sad story of the people's faithlessness to their faithful God. This leaves no place for human efforts to gloss over sin and insinuate sinners back into God's presence.

Thus a new element is introduced in verse 9: **The Lord our God is merciful and forgiving**. The word 'merciful' (*rahamin*) is frequently used in contexts of family love. Perhaps the most useful example to illustrate this is Jeremiah 31:20: 'Is not Ephraim my dear son, the child in whom I delight? Though I often speak against him, I still remember him. Therefore my heart yearns for him; I have great compassion for him, declares the LORD.' In that verse, 'compassion' is the word here translated 'mercy'. This mercy and compassion results not simply in God having kindly feelings for us but in actively pursuing our good: 'As a father has compassion on his children, so the LORD has compassion on those who fear him' (Ps. 103:13). Here that mercy expresses itself in forgiveness. The word *salah* is used only of God, as for example in Psalm 103:3, and thus suggests pardon rather than a reconciliation between equals.

Once again one of the chapter's overriding themes is emphasised. That rebellion has been particularly shown in their failure to obey God's words. And this will be directly related in the next section to disloyalty to the heart of Israel's covenant faith transmitted through Moses:

11b'Therefore the curses and sworn judgments written in the Law of Moses, the servant of God, have been poured out on us, because we have sinned against you. 12You have fulfilled the words spoken against us and against our rulers by bringing upon us great disaster. Under the whole heaven nothing has ever been done like what has been done to Jerusalem. 13Just as it is written in the Law of Moses, all this disaster has come upon us, yet we have not sought the favour of the LORD our God by turning from our sins and giving attention to your truth. 14The LORD did not hesitate to bring the disaster upon us, for the LORD our God is righteous in everything he does; yet we have not obeyed him.

This section of the prayer reminds us of the deep connection between Exodus and Exile and how the only hope in this situation is turning back to the God of Moses. The 'Law', the Torah, is the very foundation of Israel's life and experience. It is to that word that the prophet continually returned, and its predicted curses (see e.g. Lev. 26:14-45 and Deut. 28:15-68) had demonstrated its authority. These curses had been fulfilled. The consequences of disobedience to the Divine Word are awesome. They are unique: **nothing has ever been done like what has been done to Jerusalem** (v. 12).

This may well be a deliberate echo of Deuteronomy 4:32: 'Ask from one end of the heavens to the other. Has anything so great as this ever happened, or has anything like it ever been heard of?' That refers to God coming to rescue and live with his people. Thus what happened at the Exodus is not simply another tribal migration, and what happened at the Exile is not simply the fall of another city. Both are vital points in the whole plot line of God's purposes.[4] They represent the stark choice which God through Moses had laid before the people: 'See, I set before you today life and prosperity, death and destruction' (Deut. 30:15).

The theology of Chapter 1 is underlined. There we discovered that the fundamental cause of the Exile was that 'the Lord delivered Jehoiakim King of Judah into his (Nebuchadnezzar's) hand'. So here the Lord **did not hesitate to bring the disaster**

---

4 See Introduction, p. 12 for a further discussion of Exodus and Exile.

upon us. Again the theme of God's righteousness is emphasised.
The prayer continues with an emphasis now on God's rescue
of the people from Egypt.

> [15]'Now, O Lord our God, who brought your people out of Egypt
> with a mighty hand and who made for yourself a name that en-
> dures to this day, we have sinned, we have done wrong. [16]O Lord,
> in keeping with all your righteous acts, turn away your anger and
> your wrath from Jerusalem, your city, your holy hill. Our sins and
> the iniquities of our fathers have made Jerusalem and your people
> an object of scorn to all those around us.'

Having based his prayer on the character of God and shown
how this has been clearly taught in the Scriptures, Daniel now
focuses on what God does and in particular the Exodus which in
the Old Testament is the supreme historical demonstration of
God's 'mighty hand'. This is a note which sounds regularly
throughout the Psalter (see, for example, Pss. 66:5-7; 77:13-15;
much of Pss. 78; 80:7-11). We catch a glimpse of 'made for
yourself a name that endures to this day' in 1 Samuel 4:7-8 where
the Philistines, in panic at the presence of the Ark of the Covenant
with the Israelite army, cry, 'They are the gods who struck the
Egyptians.' Yet now the Exile appears to suggest that Yahweh
has been vanquished by Bel and Nebo.

This appeal to the honour of God's name recalls another
prayer in 2 Kings 19:14-19 where Hezekiah prays that God will
save Jerusalem from the Assyrians. The reason for that is 'that
all the kingdoms on earth may know that you alone, O LORD,
are God' (2 Kgs. 19:19). God had saved the city then. This prayer
asks for something beyond that; for the **city** to rise again and
thus for a renewed people to be once again those who know
God's name. Particular emphasis is placed on the **holy hill**, which
is Zion, 'the joy of the whole earth' (Ps. 48:2). As we have
noticed, Chapters 1 and 5 both make reference to the sacred
vessels removed from the Temple and here again is underlined
the fact that Jerusalem is special because God's name and honour
are associated with it.

Who God is and what God does is thus the great theme of this prayer and in its final section Daniel depends utterly on this for the answer:

> [17]'Now, our God, hear the prayers and petitions of your servant. For your sake, O Lord, look with favour on your desolate sanctuary. [18]Give ear, O God, and hear; open your eyes and see the desolation of the city that bears your Name. We do not make requests of you because we are righteous, but because of your great mercy. [19]O Lord, listen! O Lord forgive! O Lord hear and act! For your sake, O my God, do not delay, because your city and your people bear your Name.'

A frequent cry in the Psalms is 'How long, O Lord?' Here Daniel is convinced that this prayer is about to be answered and that God is about to act in fulfilment of his promise. Like the rest of the prayer, this final section is saturated in the language of earlier Scriptures. Reference Bibles list many allusions, particularly to the Psalms as well as Jeremiah and other passages. The emphasis throughout is on God's integrity and the honour of his Name. In verse 17, the phrase translated **look with favour** is in fact 'make your face shine', which is a deliberate echo of the Aaronic blessing in Numbers 6:24-26. The city and sanctuary are **desolate** (vv. 17, 18), a word which implies destruction and its consequent lack of inhabitants. The word occurs in Leviticus 26:22 and 43 as a punishment for disobedience as well as in a similar context in Jeremiah 4:27 and in Amos 7:9. The prophetic words had been amply fulfilled.

But those same prophets had spoken of a new dawn beyond the desolation which would happen because of the faithfulness of God to his covenant. In a series of impassioned verbs Daniel pleads with God to act. **Listen** does not mean that up to this point God had ignored Daniel, rather that the time to act had come. **Forgive** realises that the answer will be entirely dependent on God's grace. **Hear and act** is not an impatient demand but is a further appeal for God to vindicate the honour of his

Name. So this prayer is not only set firmly in context but is a classic example of how to pray. More will be said on this in the general comments at the end of the chapter.

The Answer (9:20-27)

Now the account takes a new turn and an answer comes while Daniel is still praying.

> 20While I was speaking and praying, confessing my sin and the sin of my people Israel and making my request to the LORD my God for his holy hill – 21while I was still in prayer, Gabriel, the man I had seen in the earlier vision, came to me in swift flight about the time of the evening sacrifice. 22He instructed me and said to me, 'Daniel, I have now come to give you insight and understanding. 23As soon as you began to pray, an answer was given, which I have come to tell you, for you are highly esteemed. Therefore, consider the message and understand the vision.'

Before we come to the controversial passage about the seventy *sevens*, some vital issues are raised in verses 20-23. The first is that an authoritative answer comes from God, just as an authoritative word from God had inspired the prayer. Moreover, the answer was given immediately the prayer began. This underlines the sovereignty of God and refutes any idea that Daniel's prayer may have forced his hand. Yet the prayer was necessary because without it Daniel would not have been spiritually ready to receive the answer. In a use of repetition characteristic of the book, verse 20 reminds us of the important elements of the prayer and the right way to approach God.

Another significant issue is the importance of angels in the life of prayer. Angels, according to Psalm 103:20, are 'mighty ones who do his bidding, who obey his word'; Psalm 91:11 speaks of angels guarding the faithful. 2 Kings 6:13ff. tells of Elisha and his servant trapped by the Syrian army in the town of Dothan. When Elisha prays, the servant sees 'the hills full of horses and chariots of fire all around Elisha'. Elisha's prayer did not create the angels, it allowed them to be seen. And there is the great story in Acts 12 of the praying church and Peter's subsequent rescue by the angel.

All this shows the intimate involvement of God's angels with God's people on earth. A further striking example occurs in Chapter 10. This angel is Gabriel, already seen in 8:15ff. Gabriel comes to give not only reassurance but a further message. I think we will make better sense of the seventy 'sevens' if we remember that this is an interpretation of the prophecy in Jeremiah of the end of Exile, which had inspired the prayer. It is placing the Exile in a wider context in the whole unfolding story of God's purposes, of which Chapter 7 gave a panoramic view.

It is also worth noting that this visit of Gabriel is **about the time of the evening sacrifice**. But the Temple remains desolate and for those seventy years no sacrifice has been offered. Yet the realities behind these sacrifices remained and, more profoundly, the subsequent prophecy is to point to the sacrifice which is to supersede all the ancient ritual. Indeed people like Daniel and Ezekiel had to live most of their lives without these external 'means of grace', yet were in daily contact with the God of grace himself.

This visit of Gabriel is to give to Daniel further **insight and understanding,** gifts given to him long ago (1:17). This reminds us of the need of constant openness and constant asking for wisdom (see Jas. 1:5). Yet this is balanced by verse 23: **consider the message and understand the vision**. The gift of wisdom must be responded to by diligent efforts to understand. The word 'vision' (*mar'eh*) means a total experience involving hearing as well as seeing and comes close to meaning 'revelation'.

[24]'Seventy "sevens" are decreed for your people and your holy city to finish transgression, to put an end to sin, to atone for wickedness, to bring in everlasting righteousness, to seal up vision and prophecy and to anoint the most holy.'

Generally speaking this passage is taken as being by a second century author to encourage the faithful in the days of Antiochus.

It is further argued that the failure of the numbers to work out exactly is due to the author's vagueness and indeed lack of knowledge of the historical details. Before looking at possible interpretations, however, it is important to look at verse 24 which gives the reasons for the seventy 'sevens'. Gabriel very directly addresses the issues of the prayer by dealing with the Exile and its aftermath. Yet it is also made clear that the Exile can only be understood in a much longer perspective. This is shown by the use of the word 'sevens' itself. Commentators rightly draw attention to Leviticus 25:8 which speaks of 'seven sabbaths of years', and to Leviticus 26:34 where the Exile is seen as the land 'enjoying its sabbaths'. This links Exile and Exodus again and illustrates the interrelatedness of these events. However, there is an even more basic factor. Behind all biblical uses of seven lie the seven days of creation. Thus the return from Exile is not simply to be a new Exodus but a new creation and thus foreshadows the End time. The negative elements of putting away sin correspond to these elements earlier in the prayer (see vv. 7ff.), and the positive elements look to the re-establishing of the Temple but go far beyond that. Since the prayer began with God's righteousness its answer must be the establishing of that righteousness. We are told in Romans 1:17: 'In the gospel a righteousness from God is revealed.' The sealing of vision and prophecy refers to the establishing and confirming of the Word of God to Jeremiah. This is the emphasis of 2 Corinthians 1:20: 'For no matter how many promises God has made, they are "Yes" in Christ. And so through him the "Amen" is spoken by us to the glory of God.' The 'most holy' refers initially to the holy of holies, the central shrine in the Temple which housed the Ark of the Covenant. Yet that was only a symbol. As David and Ezekiel[5] make abundantly plain, the glory of God is not confined to the now desolate temple in Jerusalem anymore than it was to the tent in the desert. The true Ark is the Lord Jesus Christ who 'became flesh' and 'pitched his tent among us' (John 1:14). Thus

---

[5] In Chapter 1 of Ezekiel the vision which the prophet sees is effectively a mobile Ark of the Covenant – see also Chapter 8, especially vv. 9-22.

only in Christ can the Exile be understood.

Gabriel now continues and expounds the seventy sevens in more detail:

> 25'Know and understand this: From the issuing of the decree to restore and rebuild Jerusalem until the Anointed One, the ruler, comes, there will be seven "sevens" and sixty-two "sevens". It will be rebuilt with streets and a trench, but in times of trouble.'

Verse 24 has spoken of the entire period of the seventy 'sevens', now more detail is to be filled in. On a small scale this repeats the pattern of Chapters 7 and 8, with Chapter 7 giving the broad sweep of history and Chapter 8 focusing on a more specific period. The **decree to restore and rebuild Jerusalem** is probably that given by Cyrus in 539 BC. This will be followed by two periods: a shorter one of seven 'sevens' and a longer one of sixty-two 'sevens'. The first period would then be the time between Cyrus' decree and the completion of Jerusalem **with streets and a trench**, which did not take place until the time of Nehemiah. The **Anointed One, the ruler**, is a general term; it is used of Cyrus himself in Isaiah 45:1, and of Israel's kings and priests also. Those who see Daniel as a second century book take the first period of 'seven sevens' as effectively the Exile and the 'Anointed One' as Cyrus or Joshua the priest (see Ezra 3:2; Hag. 1:1; Zech. 3:1). The sixty-two 'sevens' take us up to 171 BC when the high priest Onias was murdered, the final seven concluding with the restoration of the Temple in 164 which symbolised the victory of God. Undoubtedly these events are illustrations of the final fulfilment but to see them as exhausting the meaning would be short-sighted.

The next important event is alluded to in verse 26.

> 26'After the sixty-two "sevens", the Anointed One will be cut off and will have nothing. The people of the ruler who will come will destroy the city and the sanctuary. The end will come like a flood: War will continue until the end, and desolations have been decreed.'

God's purposes centre in this 'Anointed One' and culminate in the final 'seven'. The Anointed One will suffer violent death – **be cut off**. Since he is also **the ruler**, the reference to Onias does not seem to fulfil this text all that well. The language is strongly reminiscent of Isaiah 53:8: 'he was cut off from the land of the living.' **And will have nothing** probably refers to the apparent total disaster which overwhelms him. The text at once becomes clearer and more mysterious in the light of the cry of dereliction: 'My God, my God why have you forsaken me?' **The people of the ruler** can hardly be Antiochus because, although he caused much havoc, he did not destroy either city or Temple (see 1 Macc. 1:31, 38). Indeed, he rebuilt much of it (1 Macc. 1:32). So it is more natural to see this as referring to the destruction of Jerusalem in AD 70 by the Romans under Titus. This is another reminder that the Exile did not exhaust the desolation which came upon Jerusalem. The use of words such as **flood** and **desolations** emphasise the totality of the destruction.

But there is more to come:

> [27]'He will confirm a covenant with many for one "seven". In the middle of the "seven" he will put an end to sacrifice and offering. And on a wing[6] of the temple he will set up an abomination that causes desolation, until the end that is decreed is poured out on him.'

The first question to decide is who is 'he' in the first sentence. Those who argue for a second century date say it is Antiochus and speak of how apostate Jews co-operated with him (see 1 Macc. 1:11-15). Others see it as the Antichrist, the final fulfilment of the little horn of Daniel 7. It is also possible to see verses 26 and 27 as parallel accounts of the same events in which case the 'Anointed One' would be the subject, which would mean that the second half, like the second half of verse 26, refers to Titus who began another and more terrible exile. He **confirms** a covenant rather than makes a new one. Now if it is the Messiah

---

[6] The 'wing' is taken by many to be a pinnacle of the temple, but it may also apply to the wing-like corners or horns of the altar. See Goldingay, p. 263.

who is the subject, the covenant would be the everlasting one sealed at Calvary.

The NIV translation makes it appear that in the second half of the verse the subject is the same as the first – **he will set up an abomination**. But a more literal rendering is 'upon the wing shall be an abomination'. If my suggestion that verses 26 and 27 are parallel is correct, then we can see this as corresponding to the activities of the 'people of the ruler' in the earlier verse. The sacrifices ceased after Christ's death, not in the sense that they are no longer offered, but in the sense that 'He appeared once for all at the end of the ages to do away with sin by the sacrifice of himself' (Heb. 9:26). The imagery of the desolation, as we have seen, has many references. The first belongs in the Exile itself with the desolation of Jerusalem and the desecrating of the Temple vessels (see Chapter 5). Then it refers to the activities of Antiochus. Then it refers to the sack of the city by Titus in AD 70 and indeed it has a broader application to all persecutions and attack on God's people throughout history.

The so-called 'Dispensational'[7] interpretation accepts the Messianic interpretation but argues that there is a gap between the 69th and 70th weeks. This parenthesis is the Church Age which runs from the death of Christ until his coming. This view argues that the natural reading of verse 26 is that the death of the Messiah and the destruction of the city happen before rather than during the 70th week. If, however, we take the events of verse 27 as parallel to rather than following those of verse 26, this is unnecessary. This view further takes the subject in verse 27 as the Antichrist who will preside during the Great Tribulation which will intervene between the coming of Christ for his people and the subsequent coming to reign on earth during the Millennium.

---

[7] Dispensationalism is a total view of biblical interpretation. A reasonably straightforward but critical view of this teaching can be found in *Prophecy and the Church* by O. T. Allis (Philadelphia, 1945). A much briefer recent account which relates especially to Revelation 20 can be found in *When Jesus Returns* by J. David Pawson (Hodder & Stoughton, 1995) pp. 262-266.

Now, while believing the Dispensational view to be mistaken, yet it must be remembered that the great crisis moments of history, whether Exile, the time of Antiochus or the time of Titus, are all moments of judgment. The enemies of God whether Babylon, Persia, Greece, Rome or their modern counterparts are a manifestation of the devilish forces which emerge throughout history (see Chapter 7). Thus, although I believe that these verses are best understood as relating to Christ's coming and the sack of Jerusalem some forty years later in AD 70, they also foreshadow the End. This is seen especially clearly in the New Testament in the Olivet Discourse or 'Little Apocalypse' (Matt. 24; Mark 13 and Luke 21). There what our Lord says seems to refer both to the sack of Jerusalem and to the time of the End which that event foreshadowed.

As I write these words I have a splendid view of Durham Cathedral which appears to rise immediately behind some houses and trees at the bottom of some allotments which face our street. What cannot be seen from here is that the cathedral stands on a lofty outcrop of sandstone on the other side of the deep valley of the River Wear. So it is that the Old Testament prophets, as they looked into the future, did not clearly distinguish between the first and second Comings of Christ. In a profound sense, of course, they were right, in that both comings are part of the great invasion of God into human affairs to win a people for his Name and to restore his creation. All this depends on the great events of Christ's death and resurrection which were to take place in the seventh week, and it is on these events and not on complicated arithmetical calculations that our emphasis must lie.

The chapter thus fits comfortably into the developing pattern of the book. The heart of the book, Chapters 2:4–7:28, written in the international language Aramaic, concentrates on world history and the broad sweep of God's purposes. Chapter 1 fits the destiny of the Jews, that nation through whom these purposes were to be accomplished, into that frame. Chapters 8–12, again in Hebrew, concentrate on Jewish history in particular, with the 'Beautiful Land' (8:9, 11:41) as the focus.

General Comments

Reference has already been made to this chapter's use of the theme of the relationship between the Bible and prayer and it would be worth reflecting further on these two interrelated subjects.

The Bible

A number of significant points about the nature of Scripture emerge in this passage.

1. We have a fascinating glimpse of the formation of the canon of Scripture. The recent (for Daniel) prophecy of Jeremiah is given the same authority as the foundational writings of Moses. A useful parallel occurs in 2 Peter 3:15-16 where Peter speaks of the writings of 'our dear brother Paul' and places them on the same level as 'the other Scriptures'. Moreover as we have seen the prayer is rich with Scriptural allusions.

2. The prayer illustrates the fundamental connection between Bible reading and prayer. Only as we deepen our understanding of God as revealed in the Bible will our praying become richer and more soundly based on who God is. When I was a boy I used to be irritated by prayers which spoke of the nature of God and his mighty acts. Why could we not get on with the business of praying? However, that is the business of praying. Only because of who God is and what he does can prayer be answered. Thus knowledge of the Bible is the essential foundation for true prayer.

3. Daniel also by his use of the Bible shows a fine appreciation of his own part in the whole unfolding story of God's purposes. These purposes are chronicled in the words of the prophets (not forgetting that Moses himself is the prophet *par excellence*, see Deut. 34:10). As we have seen these prophetic words spoken in particular circumstances yet speak to other times and are always contemporary. Thus the ancient words of God through Moses

speak into the situation of Exile and its end, but these words and the words of this chapter which echo them also speak into the age of Antiochus, of Titus, and to our own day and indeed every day until the End.

4. This chapter, with the rest of the Old Testament points to Christ, 'the Anointed One, the ruler'. Only in him do the words find true fulfilment. Seen in his light, the prophecy of the seventy weeks becomes a light shining in a dark place and pointing to the triumph that lies beyond the desolations.

Prayer

Out of Daniel's study grows this great prayer which reveals so much about the theology and practice of praying.

1. The prayer is both deeply personal and yet profoundly corporate. We noticed the balance of 'my God' and 'our God'. Daniel, for most of his life, had not lived in Jerusalem. Indeed Jerusalem was no more. Yet his passionate concern (see also in Ezekiel) was for his people. Indeed his concern was not simply for the southern kingdom but for the north which was centuries before deported to Assyria. True prayer will always blend these elements and will be large and generous in its sympathies.

2. A further balance in the prayer is between the spontaneous and the liturgical. As we have seen, this prayer arises out of Daniel's own situation and represents his deepest feelings. Yet nearly every word echoes earlier Scriptures and these are the words which embody his own profound emotions. Indeed we could go further and argue that the only way to pray spontaneously is to be soaked in Scripture. This prayer is a good illustration of Paul's words in Colossians 3:16: 'Let the word of Christ dwell in you richly as you teach and admonish one another with all wisdom, and as you sing psalms, hymns and spiritual songs with gratitude in your hearts to God.'

3. Mention has already been made of the importance of angels, in this case Gabriel. Gabriel does not answer the prayer, he brings the answer. Yet he also brings reassurance and comfort. We need to recapture the sense of the importance of angels. I shall say more about this in the discussion of Chapter 10.

4. Believing in a God who answers prayer and who governs everything in no way dispenses with the need for faith. Rather prayer invites us into active participation in God's purposes. This has been touched on in the discussion of Chapter 7 and will be looked at further in Chapter 11. In prayer Daniel listens and obeys.

Thus this great chapter is a fascinating study of these most basic and irreplaceable elements of the life of faith: the Bible and prayer. It is a rare glimpse of Daniel's inner life and the spiritual force which sustained him.

Questions for further study

1. What does this chapter say about the importance of Scripture?

2. Does the chapter support liturgical prayers?

3. Does the passage about the 'Seventy Sevens' (24-27) add anything new to our understanding of the future?

10

Principalities and powers

A group of American College students, frustrated with their struggle to understand the book of Revelation, went to the gym to play basketball. After their game they noticed that the old caretaker was sitting in the corner reading. 'What you reading, Joe?', they asked. 'The book of Revelation,' he replied. 'Oh, you can't understand that.' 'Yes,' Joe replied, 'it's quite simple. Jesus wins.' Surely there is a profound truth there. Apocalyptic literature such as Revelation and Daniel contains much mystery (as we have seen especially in the discussion of the 70 weeks) but we must never lose sight of this basic truth – 'Jesus wins'. The Son of Man will come with the clouds of heaven and every knee will bow and every tongue confess that he is Lord.

With Daniel 10 we come to the final section of the book. In Chapter 10 there is the account of a vision and this is followed by a long and detailed prophecy which continues to the end of Chapter 12. A lot of the details are unclear and that is why in trying to unravel these we must not be distracted from the basic emphasis of the triumph of the Son of Man and his followers (see 12:3). The message proper takes up Chapters 11 and 12, while Chapter 10 is a record of another vision of angelic activity. We shall look at the chapter in four parts.

Introduction (10:1-3)

> [1]In the third year of Cyrus king of Persia, a revelation was given to Daniel (who was called Belteshazzar). Its message was true and it concerned a great war. The understanding of the message came to him in a vision.

We have become accustomed to time references in the book and there are a number of important features of this dating here.

There is a deliberate reminder of Chapter 1 as we reach this last phase of the book. There we have the name 'Belteshazzar' given to Daniel and the fact stated that he 'continued until the first year of Cyrus' (1:21). There is no contradiction between this and the present statement that this was the third year. The context of Chapter 1 is of Daniel's active service at court. He would by now be an old man, probably at least eighty-six, and most likely would have withdrawn from active service.

The third year of Cyrus was 537 BC, and the first group of Exiles had already returned to Jerusalem to find opposition to their building of city and temple. Questions have been raised about why Daniel himself did not return with them. There is no easy answer to this, although his advanced age is clearly a factor. We can be certain that Daniel knew God's will for his remaining time. Ferguson has a useful comment: 'What these leaders [i.e. Ezra and Nehemiah] needed most (as Moses had done before) was someone who would engage in the hidden but strategic work of prayer for the defence and advance of the kingdom of God.'[1]

This new revelation is authoritative: **Its message was true**. Yet it was painful: **it concerned a great war**. The word *ts'ba* translated 'war' is interesting. It is used in Isaiah 40:2 to describe the Exile itself. Here I suggest that it has two shades of meaning. The first is the great burden upon Daniel himself of receiving this revelation. This has been a feature of such experiences (see 7:28; 8:27). Also it probably refers to the wars in heaven alluded to in this chapter and their earthly counterparts in Chapter 11. Again we have the inextricable link of word and vision.

The circumstances of receiving the vision are now detailed.

> [2]At that time I, Daniel, mourned for three weeks. [3]I ate no choice food; no meat or wine touched my lips; and I used no lotions at all until the three weeks were over.

Since the Passover was celebrated on the first day of the first month the three weeks of mourning would include that as well as the Feast of Unleavened Bread. Now as the God of the Exodus

[1] Ferguson. p. 207.

works again to reverse the Exile Daniel is conscious that great events are afoot. Just how great these are he has already glimpsed and is about to be given further revelation.

The reference to food and wine is another reminder of Chapter 1. It is an interesting sidelight on the fact that vegetables and water were not his habitual diet but emergency rations for times of crisis. Psalm 45:7 speaks of anointing as a sign of joy which would also be inappropriate for this time.

The Vision (10:4-9)
At the end of the three weeks Daniel has a most awe-inspiring vision.

> 4On the twenty-fourth day of the first month, as I was standing on the bank of the great river, the Tigris, 5I looked up and there before me was a man dressed in linen, with a belt of the finest gold round his waist. 6His body was like chrysolite, his face like lightning, his eyes like flaming torches, his arms and legs like the gleam of burnished bronze, and his voice like the sound of a multitude.

Usually in the Old Testament, the 'Great River' when it appears alone refers to the Euphrates. Both rivers, however, are part of the exilic experience of God's people. By that river Daniel sees a majestic figure. Linen is the dress of the angelic visitants in Ezekiel 9:2, and it was the material from which priestly garments were made (Lev. 16:4). Gold is the sign of royal dignity. Who was this figure? Most commentators argue that this was an angel, perhaps Gabriel whom we met in Chapters 8 and 9. But some details and indeed the overall impression suggest something different. Lightning is characteristic of a theophany (for example, Exod. 19:16; 20:18; Ezek. 1:13-14; Ps. 18:12). Indeed the fire of God's presence at Sinai, represented also by the lamp burning in the shrine as young Samuel slept (1 Sam. 3), suggests that this figure is the Lord himself.

The closest parallel is the vision of the Son of Man in Revelation 1:12-15, the details of which correspond closely to this vision. There John on Patmos sees a glorious figure who is

not Christ as he was, not even Christ as he will be, but Christ as
he now is. That is the controlling vision of the book. The Son of
Man holds the keys of death and of the world to come. So here
I suggest that what we have is a Christophany, a pre-incarnate
appearance of the Son of God who is also the Son of Man. Thus
God himself comes to authenticate his revelation. Here the linen
then has the deeper significance that the one who wears it is a
priest who opens the way for sinful humans to return to God.
The gold and bronze emphasise solidity and tangible reality.
The voice was greater than any single human sound. Moreover,
the impact of this vision is greater than any others and this
emphasis continues in the following verses.

> [7]I, Daniel, was the only one who saw the vision; the men with me
> did not see it, but such terror overwhelmed them that they fled and
> hid themselves. [8]So I was left alone, gazing at this great vision; I
> had no strength left, my face turned deathly pale and I was help-
> less. [9]Then I heard him speaking, and as I listened to him, I fell
> into a deep sleep, my face to the ground.

Verse 7 gives a further indication that this figure is the Lord
himself. Daniel's companions, like Paul's on the road to
Damascus (Acts 9:3ff.), hear a voice and are terrified although
they see no-one. The effect on Daniel himself is to cause great
physical weakness (verse 8). It is not fun to see God. Here there
is no laughter, no jumping around, but helplessness and fear. So
overwhelming was the sight and the sound of his voice that
Daniel was overcome with sleep.

The Message (10:10-14)
Consistent with the pattern we have noticed throughout the book,
Daniel is not left to come to his senses unaided and then to work
out the meaning of the vision for himself.

> [10]A hand touched me and set me trembling on my hands and knees.
> [11]He said, 'Daniel, you who are highly esteemed, consider care-
> fully the words I am about to speak to you, and stand up, for I have

now been sent to you.' And when he said this to me, I stood up trembling.

Before the actual message is delivered, Daniel is given reassurance. The touch reminds us of the many occasions on which Jesus touched lepers and other outcasts, thereby showing solidarity and support. Further, this touch enabled Daniel to begin to get up, although he was still fearful. Yet, as in the healing miracles of Jesus, the touch was the prelude to the word, because the Lord has come to give to Daniel not only reassurance but revelation.

Daniel is again described as 'highly esteemed' or 'greatly beloved'. We may compare this with John as 'the disciple whom Jesus loved'. Another such phrase is used of Abraham who is called 'friend of God' (Isa. 41:8) and of Moses 'whom the LORD knew face to face' (Deut. 34:10). These, and others, were all privileged to hear the Divine message, but that hearing was a costly and painful business. Once again there is to come a revelation which will need all Daniel's attention and careful consideration, and thus Daniel, still trembling, stands up.

[12]Then he continued, 'Do not be afraid, Daniel. Since the first day that you set your mind to gain understanding and to humble yourself before your God, your words were heard, and I have come in response to them. [13]But the prince of the Persian kingdom resisted me twenty-one days. Then Michael, one of the chief princes, came to help me, because I was detained there with the king of Persia. [14]Now I have come to explain to you what will happen to your people in the future, for the vision concerns a time yet to come.'

The reassurance is not confined to a sympathetic touch, this is reinforced by a strengthening word. **Do not be afraid** are the words also spoken by the Risen Lord on Patmos and by the Lord himself and his angels on innumerable occasions. It is a reminder of how human Daniel was; he was not unfeeling or free from human fears, and so the Lord graciously met him at his point of need.

Then comes a passage which takes us right to the heart of prayer and its effectiveness. While prayer is not a bargaining with God where we offer our devotion as a reason for hearing us, there is a clear connection between the effectiveness of our prayers and our spiritual state. James 5:16 tells us that 'The prayer of a righteous man is powerful and effective'. There James uses the example of Elijah, and Daniel here would be another good illustration of that principle. Any idea that the prayer, however, was answered because of Daniel's merits is dispelled by his humility and confession of sin in 9:5-14 and underlined by the phrase here in verse 12, **humble yourself**. But what is undoubtedly true is that Daniel, by his deep concern for the kingdom of God, had made it possible for him to receive the heavenly visitor.

Two factors in particular had made that a possibility. We have already mentioned his humility, his sense of being totally unworthy in the presence of God. The other fact is that Daniel **set [his] mind to gain understanding**. Here we have the perfect blend of heart and mind; no vague emotional fervour on the one hand, nor an arid intellectual exercise on the other. Daniel has consistently exemplified both these qualities and is still doing so in old age. Prayer is essentially about relationships – and all good relationships involve clear thinking as well as warm affection.

But there are further fascinating revelations about the nature of answered prayer. Daniel's prayer had been heard **from the first day**, i.e. some three weeks earlier, and at that very moment the heavenly figure had started to come to him. Why then had he taken twenty-one days? Plainly this is not the time it takes to travel from heaven to earth! Rather he had been delayed by a conflict in the heavenly places. A titanic struggle was raging there of which the earthly conflicts of Persia and Greece were simply echoes. Behind each earthly power stands an angel prince.[2] Here the powerful figure who guides the destinies of

---

[2] This is not a 'late' idea introduced from Persian sources but occurs throughout the Old Testament, for example, Isaiah 24:21 speaks of Yahweh punishing 'the powers in the heavens above'.

Persia **resisted** the heavenly visitor. Then to his help comes **Michael, one of the chief princes**. This little passage shows us that prayer is no mechanical activity but involves struggle, uncertainty and faith. However convinced we may be of the final outcome, the way we experience the struggle at any given moment is unpredictable. This is why Paul says in Ephesians 6:12: 'Our struggle is not against flesh and blood, but against the rulers, against the authorities, against the powers of this dark world and against the spiritual forces of evil in the heavenly realms.' Thus to be involved in that realm, the only one where real victories can be won, we cannot and dare not neglect prayer.

The substance of the message, which is to be unfolded in Chapters 11 and 12, **concerns a time yet to come**. As we have seen often in our consideration of the previous chapters, while there is an increasing focus on the time of Antiochus, the central thrust of all the prophecies is the 'last days' and we shall explore this further in the exposition of Chapters 11 and 12.

Explanation (10:15-11:1)
This whole chapter has been an introduction to the lengthy revelation in Chapters 11 and 12, and the heavenly visitor adds a few more words of explanation of **why I have come to you**.

> [15]While he was saying this to me, I bowed with my face towards the ground and was speechless. [16]Then one who looked like a man touched my lips, and I opened my mouth and began to speak. I said to the one standing before me, 'I am overcome with anguish because of the vision, my lord, and I am helpless. [17]How can I, your servant, talk with you, my lord? My strength is gone and I can hardly breath.'

Daniel is in need of a second touch, for the experience has left him dumb. This was hardly surprising for this vision of heavenly warfare and the realm he had been in touch with by prayer must have been awe-inspiring. Even with his lifelong commitment to prayer he could scarcely have imagined until this moment just what momentous issues hung upon his intercessions. The

touching of his lips recalls Isaiah's lips touched with fire from
the altar (Isa. 6:7) which leads to cleansing and to the proclaiming
of a message. When Daniel speaks here he again expresses his
own extreme weakness and his total dependence on the Lord.
This leads to the third strengthening touch.

> [18]Again the one who looked like a man touched me and gave me
> strength. [19]'Do not be afraid, O man highly esteemed,' he said,
> 'Peace!' Be strong now; be strong.'
>   When he spoke to me, I was strengthened and said, 'Speak, my
> lord, since you have given me strength.'

Just as Elijah was strengthened more than once when in a state
of extreme weakness (1 Kgs. 19:5-8), so here Daniel is touched
and encouraged yet again. We have often noticed how the book
uses repetition for emphasis and so again we have the touch, the
strengthening word, and this time the repeated command to **be
strong**. It is the word which completes Daniel's recovery and
gives him renewed strength and the confidence to inquire further.

> [20]So he said, 'Do you know why I have come to you? Soon I will
> return to fight against the prince of Persia, and when I go, the
> prince of Greece will come, [21]but first I will tell you what is written
> in the Book of Truth. (No one supports me against them except
> Michael, your prince. [1]And in the first year of Darius the Mede, I
> took my stand to support and protect him.)'

This final part of the chapter both confirms and carries forward
the previous revelation Daniel had already seen of how the
various empires would rise and fall, but now in this final message
more detail is to be given about how this will affect God's people.
Persia will pass from the stage to be replaced by Greece. In the
midst of the clash of these great powers (the ram and the goat of
Chapter 8), the fate of a community of exiles seems unimportant.
Yet this is not so, for beside them and for them stands and fights
the Divine Messenger himself and Michael the archangel.
     There are two important elements here. One is that the God

of Israel can disclose the sequence of events before they happen. More will be said about this in the discussion of Chapter 11 but it is worth noting that this is a part of the overall securing of God's people.

Secondly, the communicating of this revelation is a necessary assurance in the conflict. The sequence of world events will be such that the coming of God's kingdom will look more and more unlikely. Thus the revelation of the future does not take away the need for faith; rather it is a vital part of that faith and a necessary stimulus to endurance. The emphasis on God's word is underlined by the reference to the 'Book of Truth'. An allusion to Psalm 139:16 is possible here: 'All the days ordained for me were written in your book before one of them came to be.' Likewise, in Malachi 3:16, the faithful in the post-exilic community are said to be recorded in 'a scroll of remembrance'.

Chapter 11:1 is probably better taken as the ending of Chapter 10 (in line with the NIV). **The first year of Darius**, already referred to in 9:1 as the inspiration of Daniel's prayer, was the year in which events were set in motion to allow the exiles to return to their homeland. What the Messenger is showing here is that this event was not simply a policy decision on the part of Cyrus and influenced by political considerations. Rather the heavenly powers have been active, and the events sovereignly ordained by God and revealed to his servant are now unfolding.

General Comments

As already noted, this chapter is a long introduction to the final revelation and as such shows the importance of what follows. Nevertheless it is also important in its own right for its revelation of the nature of reality and its insight into the heavenly world. In particular, three great realities are emphasised.

The reality of the unseen world

Behind earthly nations and events is a far greater reality. Deuteronomy 32:8-9 speaks of nations being allotted to heavenly beings: 'When the Most High gave the nations their inheritance, when he divided all mankind, he set up boundaries for the peoples according to the numbers of the sons of Israel.' This phrase 'sons of Israel', both in the Septuagint and the Dead Sea Scrolls, is rendered 'sons of God' and taken to refer to the heavenly court. This explains the often devilish manifestations of nationhood and tribalism such as the Holocaust and more recent events in Bosnia and Rwanda. The importance of angels in Scripture can scarcely be underestimated, appearing as they do in every significant part of biblical revelation. Psalm 103:20 speaks of God's angels as his 'mighty ones who do his bidding'.

The reality of conflict

What is spelled out here is the continuing reality of the conflict announced in Genesis 3:15: 'And I will put enmity between you and the woman, and between your offspring and hers; he will crush your head, and you will strike his heel.' Here the cosmic as well as the earthly dimensions of that conflict are delineated. Daniel was a most effective politician and administrator, but this realm which was revealed to him is a far more fundamental one where the real battles are fought and victories won.

The importance of this conflict is spelled out in many passages of Scripture, perhaps most clearly in Ephesians 6:12: 'For our struggle is not against flesh and blood, but against the rulers, against the authorities, against the powers of this dark world and against the spiritual forces of evil in the heavenly realms.' Any effective living for God is impossible without recognising the reality of and engaging in this conflict.

The reality of prayer

We have already seen much of Daniel's prayers in very different kinds of circumstances and now something of its impact on the unseen world is emphasised. This is a powerful appeal for believing prayer as we are shown a glimpse of the realities of the heavenly world which prayer opens to us. Above all, perhaps, it is another reminder that even the strongest faith needs to be sustained amid the harsh realities of daily living.

Questions for further study

1. What do you think is the importance of angels in the life of a believer?

2. Has reading this chapter changed your view of reality?

3. Why is there such a long introduction to the last vision?

The end is not yet

'We do not see how it could be used for a sermon or for sermons.'[1] These rather dismal words from one of the commentaries are not untypical of the attitude of many towards this chapter. Chapter 11 certainly lacks the vivid narrative interest of such Chapters as 3 and 5 or the colourful apocalyptic imagery of Chapters 7 and 8. On the one hand, most commentators dismiss it as a survey of the history of the Persian and Greek periods; on the other, conservatives such as Leupold, quoted above, agree that it is indeed genuine prophecy, but simply assert that the important thing about it was that it happened.

Against that view, however, must be set the fact that Chapter 10 is the most impressive introduction to any of the sections of the book. This is even more striking if, as already argued, the heavenly visitor is the Lord himself. Thus, especially bearing in mind that Chapter 12 is part of this long closing section, it seems likely that there is far more significance in this chapter than the above remarks suggest.

Two major issues need to be examined before looking at the details of this passage. The first is the standpoint of the chapter, i.e. how is it looking at the events and what principles govern the choice of details? The second is the relationship between prophecy and history. Is this chapter a genuine prediction of events by a sixth century author, and if so, what is the purpose?

Taking first the question of standpoint, the place to start is probably verse 16 where 'the king of the North' establishes himself in **the Beautiful Land**. The 'Beautiful Land' occurs again in verse 41 and has occurred in 8:9 as the perspective from which the events are being viewed. From that standpoint, the 'king of

---

[1] *Exposition of Daniel* (Grand Rapids: Baker Book House, 1969), p. 525 by H. C. Leupold.

the South' is the ruler of Egypt and the 'king of the North' the ruler of Syria. More will be said shortly about some of the historical details.

But why is the land 'beautiful'? The reason for this is that God placed his glory there. When we remember that this prophecy is dated in 'the third year of Cyrus' (10:1), we know that the first exiles had returned (Ezra 1). Ezekiel had seen a vision of the glory of God leaving the Temple: 'Then the glory of the LORD departed from over the threshold of the temple' (Ezek. 10:18). At the end of his prophecy he had seen it return to a renewed temple: 'the glory of the LORD filled the temple' (Ezek. 43:5). This, I believe, helps us to understand the concentration on the time of Antiochus. In the Exile the glory of God had moved to Babylon to appear to Ezekiel (Chapters 1 and 37) and many times to Daniel. The point of this, as already noted, is that Yahweh is not a local deity confined to a shrine but his glory fills heaven and earth. But what happens when Babylon infiltrates Zion and a more deadly internal régime of Exile is imposed?

One further detail is important at this point. Montgomery says: 'This chapter is the first Jewish attempt at a universal history since the Table of the Nations, Gen. 10.'[2] While not agreeing with Montgomery that this is written after the events it seems nevertheless that his underlying point is valid. As we shall see, towards the end of the chapter, the figure of Antiochus recedes and gives way to someone more sinister, so throughout the chapter there are hints that this historical period is simply a window into a greater reality. By using phrases such as the kings of the north and the south, the writer gives a universal flavour to his material.

Now to our second question, which is whether we are reading history or prophecy. Those who argue that it is historical do not necessarily deny its value. Goldingay, for example, argues that 'It is not that prediction of second-century events in the sixth century would be impossible; let its possibility be granted.'[3] Rather he maintains that God speaks to real people in real

---

[2] Montgomery, p. 421.   [3] Goldingay, p. 321.

contexts and declines to give future information since this rather takes away the need to live by faith. He further argues that this literary device of 'quasi-prophecy' was not meant to deceive and indeed would have deceived no-one. The point of the chapter is to demonstrate the rule of God in human history.

A number of considerations arise out of this. The first is that we must not press too rigidly the distinction between prophecy and history. The books we normally call 'history books' (i.e. Joshua–2 Kings, excluding Ruth) are in the Hebrew Bible known as the 'Former Prophets'. This is not simply because large sections of these books recount the activities of prophets, notably Elijah and Elisha. Rather this is history from God's standpoint, and its emphases and concerns are those of God rather than what those in power at the time think.

Moreover, history and prophecy are both necessarily selective. We can be certain that the selection of details here is valuable and profitable and that the truths are of wider application than simply to the writer's own day. The great overriding principle is that this God is not taken by surprise, this is the God 'who carries out the words of his servants and fulfils the predictions of his messengers' (Isa. 44:26). Indeed in that chapter, the incomparability of Yahweh, one of the great themes of this section of the book, is shown by the fact that no other god can 'foretell what will come' (v. 7). This is part of what his rule over history means. Paul expresses this powerfully in Romans 4:17: 'The God who gives life to the dead and calls things that are not as though they were.' Thus this chapter is an outworking of that principle.

One problem remains before we examine the chapter. If God predicts the future, does not this simply reduce humans to puppets who without being able to choose simply play out their predestined roles? This is a familiar argument and it is worth noting that to over-emphasise human freedom in effect reduces God to a puppet who simply has to underwrite human choices much in the way the Queen has to sign acts of Parliament. But both these views are too simplistic.

The first thing to be considered is the importance of the prophetic word. The word of the prophet which is the word of the Lord always summons to a choice. We have already seen how Nebuchadnezzar and Belshazzar responded to the divine word. In both cases that word was fulfilled, but in both cases the human response was an important factor in its fulfilment. In other words the events prophesied in this chapter are intimately related to the choices made and the character of the individuals concerned.

Because of this, the prophetic word has relevance beyond its immediate setting. The particular relevance will be our task to discover in the following exegesis. But some general points can be made. The first is that the normal alliances of power and politics are not excluded by the divine overruling of history, and genuine options are available. The second is that certain patterns of behaviour occur in different generations; arrogance, oppression and tyranny are not confined to the periods of the Exile or Antiochus. The third, and most important, is that prophecy ultimately relates to Christ whose kingdom is to last for ever.

With this in mind we now turn to examine the chapter.

Persia and Greece (11:2-4)

2'Now then, I tell you the truth: Three more kings will appear in Persia, and then a fourth, who will be far richer than all the others. When he has gained power by his wealth, he will stir up everyone against the kingdom of Greece. 3Then a mighty king will appear, who will rule with great power and do as he pleases. 4After he has appeared, his empire will be broken up and parcelled out towards the four winds of heaven. It will not go to his descendants, nor will it have the power he exercised, because his empire will be uprooted and given to others.'

We return here to the period symbolised in the vision of the ram and the male goat of Chapter 8 and the passing of power from Persia to Greece. What we have here in verse 2 is the briefest summary of Persian power. In a sense, the main significance of Persia in relation to 'the Beautiful Land' is the reversing of the Exile and the return of some of the exiles, which had already happened in the first year of Cyrus. As always the method is selective. The expression **Three more ... and then a fourth** is a common way of expressing a comprehensive survey in Hebrew,[4] and we will remember from Chapter 7 that the four beasts represented universal dominion. There is some controversy about who the four kings are; some arguing that they are the four Persian kings mentioned in the Bible, i.e. Cyrus, Darius, Xerxes and Artaxerxes. The fourth king is probably therefore not Xerxes, and Montgomery points out that Xerxes' wealth was not unusual among the Persian kings. He further points out that translations such as the NIV given above insert an 'against' into the text, and that more probably what is meant is that the kingdom of Greece will be aroused.[5] The fourth king is most probably Darius III the last of the Persian kings.

The 'mighty king' of verse 3 is plainly Alexander the Great and the theme of selfish power and ambition is again underlined in the phrase **do as he pleases**. Again too (as in 8:8) the swift demise of his empire and its fragmenting into four parts is mentioned in verse 4. While his half-brother Philip III and his son Alexander IV were nominally in charge, the real power passed to his four generals, the descendants of two of whom, the Ptolemies ('the king of the south') and the Seleucids ('the king of the north') were to be most significant for the Beautiful Land.

This little section has underlined the issues which are to be important for understanding the rest of the chapter. It is important to notice that the theology of history is that first enunciated in Chapter 1, thus binding the book together. In particular the important verb **given** (v. 4) is used about Alexander's empire

---

[4] Examples are in Proverbs 30:15ff. ('three things that are never satisfied, four that never say, "Enough!" '); again in verse 18 of mysteries; in verse 21 of unnatural things and in verse 29 of majesty. A similar pattern is found in Amos 1 and 2 in the oracles against the nations.

[5] Montgomery, pp. 423-424.

and this is a reminder that not only during the Exile which had just ended, but in the future human power will have a derivative quality and will not be self-generating. This is further illustrated by contrasting the verbs **will rule with great power** (v. 3) and **will be broken up** (v. 4). Alexander could not control the future. Whereas the main point of this chapter is that the God of heaven does, and when he thinks fit, he reveals something of that control to his servants.

South and North battle it out (5-20)

5'The king of the South will become strong, but one of his commanders will become even stronger than he and will rule his own kingdom with great power. 6After some years, they will become allies. The daughter of the king of the South will go to the king of the North to make an alliance, but she will not retain her power, and he and his power will not last. In those days she will be handed over, together with her royal escort and her father and the one who supported her.

7'One from her family line will arise to take her place. He will attack the forces of the king of the North and enter his fortress; he will fight against them and be victorious. 8He will also seize their gods, their metal images and their valuable articles of silver and gold and carry them off to Egypt. For some years he will leave the king of the North alone. 9Then the king of the North will invade the realm of the king of the South but will retreat to his own country. 10His sons will prepare for war and assemble a great army, which will sweep on like an irresistible flood and carry the battle as far as his fortress.

11'Then the king of the South will march out in rage and fight against the king of the North, who will raise a large army, but it will be defeated. 12When the army is carried off, the king of the South will be filled with pride and will slaughter many thousands, yet he will not remain triumphant. 13For the king of the North will muster another army, larger than the first; and after several years, he will advance with a huge army fully equipped.

14'In those times many will rise against the king of the South. The violent men among your own people will rebel in fulfilment of the vision, but without success. [15]Then the king of the North will come and build up siege ramps and will capture a fortified city. The forces of the South will be powerless to resist; even their best troops will not have the strength to stand. [16]The invader will do as he pleases; no-one will be able to stand against him. He will establish himself in the Beautiful Land and will have the power to destroy it. [17]He will determine to come with the might of his entire kingdom and will make an alliance with the king of the South. And he will give him a daughter in marriage in order to overthrow the kingdom, but his plans will not succeed or help him. [18]Then he will turn his attention to the coastlands and will take many of them, but a commander will put an end to his insolence and will turn his insolence back upon him. [19]After this, he will turn back towards the fortresses of his own country but will stumble and fall, to be seen no more.

[20]'His successor will send out a tax collector to maintain the royal splendour. In a few years, however, he will be destroyed, yet not in anger or in battle.'

The chapter now outlines some of the events between the demise of Alexander's empire and the rise of Antiochus Epiphanes. The **king of the South** is a generic term for the king of Egypt, and **the king of the North** for the king of Syria. It might be helpful for ease of reference to give a list at this point of the two dynasties alluded to in this chapter:

The South (Ptolemies in Egypt)	The North (Seleucids in Syria)
Ptolemy I (Soter) 323-285	Seleucus I (Nicator) 312-280
Ptolemy II (Philadelphia) 285-246	Antiochus I (Soter) 280-261
Ptolemy III (Euergetes) 246-221	Antiochus II (Theos) 261-246
Ptolemy IV (Philopator) 221-203	Seleucus II (Callinicus) 246-226
Ptolemy V (Epiphanes) 203-181	Seleucus III (Ceraunus) 226-223
Ptolemy VI (Philometor) 181-145	Antiochus III (Magnus) 223-187
	Seleucus IV (Philopator) 187-175
	Antiochus IV (Epiphanes) 175-163

Thus 'the king of the South' (v. 5) is Ptolemy I and the commander who **will become even stronger than he** is Seleucus, first Ptolemy's ally and later his rival. Indeed Seleucus I established an empire greater than Ptolemy's and indeed the greatest of the post-Alexander kingdoms.

In the manner of this chapter, which is selecting and telescoping historical events, verse 6 introduces a new theme of marriage alliance. We have now reached about 250 BC and the reference is probably to the marriage of Antiochus II and Berenice, daughter of Ptolemy II. Antiochus was already married but divorced his wife Laodice. However, after two years, Antiochus returned to Laodice, but she had him poisoned. She also arranged for Berenice, her son, and much of her Egyptian entourage to be murdered which left the way clear for Seleucus II (Callinicus) to ascend the throne.

The struggle continued when Berenice's brother, Ptolemy III, (Euergetes) became king of Egypt. He was **one from her family line** and he vigorously campaigned against Seleucus Callinicus. Verse 8 with its reference to Ptolemy seizing the images of gods is a reminder of Chapters 1 and 5 and the significance of temple vessels as a sign of the conqueror's power. Seleucus, of course, fought back but had to retreat. Verse 10 speaks of further campaigns by his successors; Seleucus III and Antiochus III carried on the conflict and with them the tide begins to flow in favour of the northern kingdom. Not that this is immediately apparent because Ptolemy IV (Philopater) **will march out in rage** (v. 12) and join battle at Raphia in 217 BC. Ptolemy won this battle but failed to press home his advantage and the victory was not consolidated. Moreover the ominous phrase **filled with pride** reminds the reader of Nebuchadnezzar and Belshazzar and creates the expectation of his downfall.

By verse 13 'the king of the North' is now Antiochus III (see table of dates) who earned for himself the title 'the Great' because of his vigorous campaigning and making up lost ground after his defeat at Raphia. He raised a huge army to attack Egypt again, an enterprise in which he was helped by internal uprisings against Ptolemy. It is at this point that the writer's perspective again becomes plain because **violent men from among your own people** (v. 14) take a hand in the struggle. Plainly much of the fighting referred to in these verses must have taken place in 'the Beautiful Land' and it is hardly surprising that some of the Jewish community should have come involved. The reference is obscure but it is plain that various factions were fighting among themselves. They may have been adherents of the rival High Priests, Onias and Tobias, who claim to be led by a 'vision' but one which events prove to be illusory.

In any case the initiative remains with Antiochus who captures Sidon, the **fortified city** of verse 15. Or at least it seems that the initiative lies with him until verse 16 restores the perspective. The invader will **do as he pleases**, and we now know that this is the prelude to the downfall of every tyrant we have met in Daniel. He vaunts himself in 'the Beautiful Land' and thus like Nebuchadnezzar, Belshazzar, Alexander the Great and many others he defies God himself.

Part, however, of Antiochus' success is that he is a diplomat as well as a general, and for the second time in these verses the topic of marriage alliances is introduced. **He will determine to come with the might of his entire kingdom** (v. 17) probably means he will press home his advantage, and he does this by arranging the marriage of his daughter Cleopatra to Ptolemy V. This failed, however, because Cleopatra became totally loyal to her husband, in fact succeeding him as regent and encouraging Egypt to form an alliance with the rising power of Rome.

Antiochus' fortunes were now on a downward course. He **turned his attention to the coastlands** (v. 18), seizing many of the cities of Asia Minor and campaigning as far as Greece itself. This career of conquest is abruptly halted by **a commander**, the Roman Lucius Cornelius Scipio who defeated him at Magnesia near Smyrna in 190 BC. The reference to his **insolence** is another reminder of the arrogance of human power which is such a feature of tyrants in the book of Daniel. Antiochus then returned to Syria, and like Sennacherib before him (2 Kgs. 19:36) was assassinated and thus came to an ignominious end.

This section is rounded off in verse 20 by **his successor**, Seleucus IV, whose reign was brief and inglorious. Not surprisingly, the unending wars of Antiochus had emptied the treasury and thus Seleucus **sent out a tax collector**. This was his chancellor Heliodorus who tried to rifle the Temple treasury in Jerusalem (see 2 Macc. 3). Heliodorus apparently turned against Seleucus and had him murdered and thus his twelve year reign ended not in glory on the battlefield but in assassination.

It would be useful at this point to pause and make some general observations on the first part of the chapter. Reasons have already been given for regarding this chapter as prophecy rather than potted history. But the reader may well be wondering if there is any point in the narration of these events other than it is an accurate account of what happened. It seems to me, however, that we have a brilliant reminder of the major themes of the book as well as the indispensable groundwork for the rest of the prophecy. Moreover we have important considerations about the nature of prophecy and the relationship of human freedom to divine sovereignty.

The basic objection made regarding this chapter (or indeed Isaiah 40–66) as genuine prophecy is that such prediction ignores human freedom and reduces human beings to mere robots doomed to carry out their part in an already determined scenario. Perhaps the most cogent expression of this view is by Lester Grabbe of Hull University:

> Perhaps one can argue for an overall divine control of history and/
> or the universe while allowing individual freedom, but a detailed
> prophecy such as Daniel 11 would render free choice impossible.
> Only if the Ptolemies and Seleucids were mere puppets in the hand
> of God could such a prophecy be made.[6]

What I want to argue now is that in a way characteristic of the book as a whole, we have a most skilful and deliberate balancing of divine sovereignty and human freedom.

These verses highlight the two passions, ambition and love,

---

[6] L. L. Grabbe: 'Fundamentalism and Scholarship: The Case of Daniel' in *Scripture: Meaning and Method* (Essays presented to A. T. Hanson ed. B. P. Thompson, Hull University Press, 1987), p. 137.

which more than any other have shaped the course of human history in every century. Time and again words such as 'become strong', 'do as he pleases' highlight the urge for power which is at the root of every régime in history. Yet another force, more potent yet, love, surfaces in the two accounts of marriage alliances (vv. 6 and 17). Indeed the latter example shows love overturning the machinations of politics when Antiochus' daughter falls in love with the husband arranged for her and encourages him in his stand against her father.

The fact that it is ambition and love which the author chose to dwell on shows that he was well aware of the interplay of destiny and choice at the heart of his prophecy. All the political and military manoeuvres were real enough; Alexander did not win his smashing victories by being passive. Similarly, the love stories doubtless followed a tortuous course, with choices having to be made at every stage. The exact relationship of these choices to the overall providence of God remains a mystery but no more so than at any other period of history. At every stage humans then as now are presented with genuine alternatives.

Moreover, the events and personalities of these verses show another characteristic of prophecy, i.e. the general nature of the comments which could apply to more than one situation. This is to become even more marked as the chapter proceeds. Thus there is difference of opinion as to whether the fourth king of Persia (v. 2) is Xerxes or the last king of the Persian empire, Darius III. Similarly verse 15 could be the defeat of Ptolemy at Panium in 198 BC or Gaza in 201 BC.[7] Since prophecy concerns the end, especially the ultimate end, persons and events of a similar nature keep on occurring and these foreshadow the final outcome.

As we approach the end of the book we see unfolding the pattern of history already seen when the young and vigorous Nebuchadnezzar had destroyed Assyria and brought the tiny kingdom of Judah to an end. Yet we also noted that it was the Lord who delivered King Jehoiakim of Judah into his hand. Here Daniel is being shown that this pattern will recur in the times

---

[7] See Baldwin, p. 191.

after his day and indeed until the End. Thus this is a message for believers in every age.

Antiochus Epiphanes emerges (11:21-35)

With Seleucus IV out of the way Antiochus Epiphanes, the figure who has been so prominent from Chapter 7 onwards, emerges centre stage. He was Seleucus' brother and the steps by which he came to power are uncertain. We shall again look at the details of the verses before commenting on the reasons for this concentration on Antiochus.

> 21'He will be succeeded by a contemptible person who has not been given the honour of royalty. He will invade the kingdom when its people feel secure, and he will seize it through intrigue. 22Then an overwhelming army will be swept away before him; both it and a prince of the covenant will be destroyed. 23After coming to an agreement with him, he will act deceitfully, and with only a few people he will rise to power. 24When the richest provinces feel secure, he will invade them and will achieve what neither his fathers nor his forefathers did. He will distribute plunder, loot and wealth among his followers. He will plot the overthrow of fortresses – but only for a time.'

In his early years Antiochus had a regent, probably his nephew, but the young man was murdered and then he was in a supreme control. The **overwhelming army** (v. 22) is most probably a general reference to the conflicts with Egypt which were to be a feature of his reign and thus anticipates his various military victories. An aspect of his anti-Egyptian policy is the destruction of **a prince of the covenant**, who is usually taken to be the High Priest Onias III, removed from his position because of his pro-Egyptian policies and replaced by Jason, one of Antiochus' cronies. Baldwin rightly points out that this marks the interference of the state in spiritual matters.[8] This is, of course, not the first example in the book; Chapters 3 and 6 show how both the Babylonian and Persian states also demanded at times the total

---

[8] Baldwin, p. 192.

allegiance which belonged to God alone.

Verse 23a is probably better translated **and he shall make alliances**, and refers to the playing off one party against another which was such a feature of Antiochus régime and which enabled him to come to power **with only a few people**. Verse 24 is difficult to translate. The NIV takes it as invasions of Antiochus which result in plunder. However, it could as well mean that he comes to the richest parts of the land and lavishes presents on those who support him. The general sense, however, is clear enough: Antiochus manipulates the wealthy and powerful to further his ends.[9] Meanwhile he plots **the overthrow of fortresses** which probably refers to his coming attack on Egypt. Yet all these intrigues are **only for a time**. The God revealed in Chapter 7, who 'gives' power, will not allow him to go on for ever.

It is hardly surprising that Antiochus should want to invade and, if possible, conquer Egypt. This ancient land, though now long past its greatest days, always exercised an irresistible fascination for 'the kings of the North'.[10]

> [25]'With a large army he will stir up his strength and courage against the king of the South. The king of the South will wage war with a large and very powerful army, but he will not be able to stand because of the plots devised against him. [26]Those who eat from the king's provisions will try to destroy him; his army will be swept away, and many will fall in battle. [27]The two kings, with their hearts bent on evil, will sit at the same table and lie to each other, but to no avail, because an end will still come at the appointed time. [28]The king of the North will return to his own country with great wealth, but his heart will be set against the holy covenant. He will take action against it and then return to his own country.'

---

[9] For a discussion of the linguistic issues involved see Montgomery, pp. 452-453.

[10] Examples of this are the so-called 'Hyksos kings' from somewhere in the Syria/Palestine area around 1700 BC and the attempts of the Assyrian king Esarhaddon to conquer Egypt in 675 BC.

The invasion of Egypt took place in 170 BC and, by a character-istic combination of military expertise and internal intrigues at the Egyptian court, Antiochus won a victory. The various intrigues led to a round table conference between him and Ptolemy V which was marked by mutual deceit. Yet neither military tactics nor devious diplomacy could prevent the end coming at the appointed time (v. 27). As I have emphasised already, this does not mean that Antiochus and the other participants were puppets, rather that only what is built on truth and integrity has enduring quality.

On his return from Egypt, Antiochus raided the temple in Jerusalem – **his heart will be set against the holy covenant**.

Antiochus' ambitions lead to a further invasion of Egypt.

> [29]'At the appointed time he will invade the South again, but this time the outcome will be different from what it was before. [30]Ships of the western coastlands will oppose him, and he will lose heart. Then he will turn back and vent his fury against the holy cov-enant. He will return and show favour to those who forsake the holy covenant.'

The second invasion of Egypt followed in 168 – **at the appointed time**. This time, however, he was thwarted by the **ships of the western coastlands**. This refers to the Romans who now be-come involved in the situation. As Antiochus was besieging Alexandria he was confronted by the Roman consul Gaius Popilius Laenas who demanded that he withdraw from Egypt. When Antiochus hesitated, the consul drew a circle round him in the sand and demanded an answer before he left it.[11] Humili-ated and furious Antiochus had to comply.

This fury had to find an outlet and he turned again against **the holy covenant**. Initially he sent one of his commanders, Apollonius, from Asia Minor to Jerusalem to suppress those loyal to God's covenant and encourage those opposed to it. A more detailed account of these events can be found in 1 Maccabees 1 and 2 Maccabees 5.

---

[11] This is described by the Roman historian Livy. xiv 1.1ff.

The situation rapidly deteriorates:

> [31]'His armed forces will rise up to desecrate the temple fortress and will abolish the daily sacrifice. Then they will set up the abomination that causes desolation. [32]With flattery he will corrupt those who have violated the covenant, but the people who know their God will firmly resist him.'

Here we have a summary of the events which culminated in the desecration of the Temple in 167 BC, and which we have encountered already in 8:11 and 9:27. The suspension of daily sacrifices, the heartbeat of the community's life of faith, was the prelude to the desolating abomination, events also recorded in 1 Maccabees 1:54. An altar to or possibly an image of Zeus was set up on the altar of burnt offering.

Antiochus also continues his policy of flattery. Presumably some of the Jews who had been favourable to his Hellenising policies were shocked at the desecration of the Temple, but were won over by skilful argument and thus become apostate, a better description than the NIV's **corrupt**. However **the people who know their God** do not capitulate either to terror or flattery. This phrase is close to the heart of the message of the whole book. Daniel himself is the supreme example of such people and his three friends are notable heroes of the faith.

> [33]'Those who are wise will instruct many, though for a time they will fall by the sword or be burned or captured or plundered. [34]When they fall, they will receive a little help, and many who are not sincere will join them. [35]Some of the wise will stumble, so that they may be refined, purified and made spotless until the time of the end, for it will still come at the appointed time.'

Those who are wise (Hebrew *Maskilim*) are often identified with a specific religious group, namely the 'Hasidim' of 1 Maccabees 2:42, the ancestors of the Pharisees who were prominent in support of Judas Maccabaeus. However, that narrowing of the term to a particular group does not fit the text especially well and it is better to relate it to what the book itself says. Back in Chapter 1 (see vv. 4 and 17) God had given wisdom to Daniel and his friends, a wisdom abundantly exemplified in the stories of Chapters 1–6, both in the ability to understand the times and operate skilfully in high politics. In Chapter 12 the wise are 'those who lead many to righteousness' (v. 3) and those who understand (v. 10). Essentially they are the same as **the people who know their God** (v. 32); that is, in this particular context, those who already by faith know that God will be God and that one day all the world will know it.

They **will instruct many** presumably means that they will teach the Torah and, like the prophets, exhort people to turn back to God. But, unlike Chapters 3 and 6, they will not be rescued from fire and sword and will give their lives.

Verse 34 contains the interesting phrase, **they will receive a little help**, which presumably refers to the resistance movement under the great Judas Maccabaeus. This is not so much disparagement as being put in the true light. In keeping with the theology of the book the sovereignty of God and his throne towering above the sea of the nations is their true refuge and strength. Yet it is not dismissed entirely. Judas and his followers were not mere puppets and what they did was valuable though limited. One of these limitations is referred to later in the verse: **many who are not sincere will join them**. This probably refers to fair-weather friends who joined the Maccabaean resistance once the bandwagon was rolling and there was the prospect of success. This would be an unlikely standpoint for an author writing in the Maccabaean age itself and is more characteristic of a genuine prophecy.

Some of the wise will stumble (v. 35). The meaning is not entirely clear. Some, e.g. Montgomery[12], take this as referring to their death, others, e.g. Ferguson[13], take it as meaning they fall away. In either case the meaning of the rest of the verse is unaltered. This time of trouble is to be one of testing and refining. Many of the commentators refer to a similar passage in

---

[12] Montgomery, p. 459.   [13] Ferguson, p. 231.

Revelation 7:14: 'These are they who have come out of the great tribulation; they have washed their robes and made them white in the blood of the Lamb.' Again **the time of the end** and the providential control of history is emphasised.

The character of Antiochus (11:36-39)
Here the passage begins to probe more deeply into the nature of Antiochus and this is to lead to a passage where the focus begins to move from him to a yet more sinister figure.

> [36]'The king will do as he pleases. He will exalt and magnify himself above every god and will say unheard-of things against the God of gods. He will be successful until the time of wrath is completed, for what has been determined must take place. [37]He will show no regard for the gods of his fathers or for the one desired by women, nor will he regard any god, but will exalt himself above them all. [38]Instead of them, he will honour a god of fortresses; a god unknown to his fathers he will honour with gold and silver, with precious stones and costly gifts. [39]He will attack the mightiest fortresses with the help of a foreign god and will greatly honour those who acknowledge him. He will make them rulers over many people and will distribute the land at a price.'

Antiochus behaved as if he were a god; calling himself 'Theos Epiphanes' – the god manifest on his coins. This presumptuous arrogance echoes the mysterious figures of the king of Babylon in Isaiah 14:12-15 who wanted to ascend to heaven and raise his throne 'above the stars of God', and the ruler of Tyre in Ezekiel 28 who says, 'I am a god; I sit on the throne of a god' (v. 2). This is the theme of Genesis 3 and the words of the serpent in verse 5: 'You will be like God.' This is echoed here in verse 36: **will do as he pleases**, which leads into an overview of Antiochus' career and personality which are simply a window into a greater reality of evil. Goldingay points out that the verbs 'exalt and magnify himself' are words used of God and that whoever aspires to such honours will be judged.[14] The next phrase, **will say unheard-of things against the God of gods**, identifies Antiochus

---

[14] Goldingay, p. 304.

as the little horn who speaks boastfully (7:8, 20). Yet all this has an appointed end; judgment will come.

Verses 37 and 38 develop this theme of Antiochus' attitude to the gods. Since he claims to be a god he is hardly likely to be interested in traditional religion: **he will show no regard for the gods of his fathers.** **The one desired by women** is often taken to refer to Tammuz, a handsome god who died and rose again, and is referred to in Ezekiel 8:14 ('women mourning for Tammuz'). In effect, Antiochus is an atheist who worships only himself.

It thus seems surprising that **he will honour a god of fortresses.** Some commentators identify this god with the citadel god Jupiter Capitlinius. However, it is much more likely that Antiochus here is seen as worshipping the god of militarism, the terrifying fourth beast with iron teeth which crushed, devoured and trampled underfoot (7:7, 19). Swollen with arrogance, he will lavish all his wealth on military conquests.

Verse 39 is obscure in its details and is difficult to fit into what is known of Antiochus' campaigns. There may be an allusion to Antiochus' settling a colony of Syrian soldiers in Jerusalem. However, we now come to the point where we must consider whether we are moving away from Antiochus himself, moving in fact to the figure of the Antichrist, the final embodiment of evil. This raises a basic question of interpretation. Are we right to 'read back', as many would have it, Christian concepts into the Old Testament? Essentially this is the question about who the Old Testament was written for? Clearly it was addressed to contemporaries, as the Word of God always is, but equally clearly, if the interpretation advocated in this commentary is right, it also addresses later generations and more particularly focuses on 'the last days', i.e. the time beginning with the coming of Christ and lasting until he comes again. There is not space here for a full discussion of this matter, but one striking passage from Hebrews is relevant here. In Chapter 9:8 in his discussion of how Christ has blazed his way into the Most Holy Place for us, the author writes: 'The Holy Spirit was showing by this that the way into the Most Holy Place had not yet been disclosed as long as the first tabernacle was still standing.' This makes the staggering claim that the Old Testament is even more relevant for us than it was for its first readers.

Thus this passage is multi-layered. Drawing some incidents from the despicable career of Antiochus Epiphanes, the heavenly messenger speaks to the faithful at the end of the Exile, those of the generation who endured the tyrant himself and all future generations until the end. This is the way the New Testament takes these passages. Thus in Matthew 24:15, Jesus says: 'So when you see standing in the holy place "the abomination that causes desolation", spoken of through the prophet Daniel – let the reader understand.' Here, Jesus speaks of something yet future, something to be partially fulfilled in 70 AD, when the Romans sacked the city, already partially fulfilled in the time of Antiochus, but to be finally fulfilled just before the Son of Man comes with the clouds of heaven. In the comments on Chapter 9 I already noted that the great moments of history are all moments of judgment and at each of these moments, just as there are figures such as Daniel who reflect Christ, so there are those such as Belshazzar and Antiochus who are precursors of the Antichrist – 'even now many antichrists have come' (1 John 2:18).

The alternative explanation, adopted by most commentators,[15] is that by verse 39 the author has reached his own period and writes a pseudo-prophecy of how the tyrant will meet his end. Since the period covered in verses 40-45 was still future to him he made many errors, most of the events cannot be found in historical records, and Antiochus died not in Palestine but Syria. However, if the prophetic nature of the whole chapter is accepted, these closing verses are a vital part of the unfolding panorama. We shall therefore examine the final verses before making some concluding remarks on the passage in general.

The time of the end (11:40-45)

40'At the time of the end the king of the South will engage him in battle, and the king of the North will storm out against him with

---

[15] For a useful summary, see Montgomery, pp. 468-470.

chariots and cavalry and a great fleet of ships. He will invade many
countries and sweep through them like a flood. ⁴¹He will also invade the Beautiful Land. Many countries will fall, but Edom, Moab
and the leaders of Ammon will be delivered from his hand. ⁴²He
will extend his power over many countries; Egypt will not escape.
⁴³He will gain control of the treasures of gold and silver and all the
riches of Egypt, with the Libyans and Nubians in submission. ⁴⁴But
reports from the east and north will alarm him, and he will set out
in a great rage to destroy and annihilate many. ⁴⁵He will pitch his
royal tents between the seas at the beautiful holy mountain. Yet he
will come to his end, and no-one will help him.'

The **time of the end** means initially the end of the reign of
Antiochus; but, as we have seen, this is simply a window into
the greater reality of the end of all things. Moreover, the battle
imagery goes well beyond merely military engagements; as we
have already seen in Chapter 10, great conflicts are being waged
by the armies of heaven. Once again, as in verse 10, imagery of
an overwhelming flood is used, linking this with earlier invaders
such as the Assyrians. The reference to **the Beautiful Land** is a
further reminder of the perspective of this chapter. This is the
land whose very existence had seemed in doubt at the Exile and
would so again many times. The fact that the neighbouring
enemies – Edom, Moab and Ammon – would escape reminds
us of the beginning of the Exile when these nations had mocked
Israel. (A fuller account of that can be found in Ezekiel 25.)
Mighty Egypt along with Nubia and Libya will be overthrown.
Plainly what we have here is a deliberate evocation of these
nations whose destinies had over the millennia been involved
with that of Israel.

    This impression is confirmed in verse 44: **But reports from
the east and the north will alarm him** recalls the words of
Isaiah about Sennacherib in 37:7: 'he will return to his own
country and there I will have him cut down with the sword.'
The final battle will be in the Beautiful Land and there evil will
finally be destroyed. The reference to the seas and the holy
mountain is most significant. The seas were the place from which

the beasts emerged; the holy mountain is Zion, the joy of the whole earth, the city of the living God. Thus the conflict is of cosmic dimensions; Exodus and Exile with all their significance pointed beyond themselves to the far greater conflicts in the heavenly realms. This is about to be confirmed by the appearance of Michael in 12:1. The oppressor who seemed so strong is to vanish, helpless, friendless and futile.

General Comments

At various points in our study of this chapter we have paused to make more general observations. Now we must try to tie the many threads together. We have already rejected the view that this is history thinly disguised as prophecy and have taken it as a genuine unfolding of future events with a powerful theological message. However, we have also found wanting the kind of conservative view that sees the only interest in the chapter being that the events actually happened. Yet it is a chapter seldom preached on[16] and in my own preaching and teaching of Daniel up to now I have had little to say about it. However, one of the advantages of writing a commentary is that one is obliged to tackle seriously passages either ignored or only lightly touched on and it has become increasingly clear to me that this chapter is one of the most important in the whole book. Four particular issues call for comment.

1. The first is that, in spite of appearances, this is a very practical chapter. In many ways the emphasis of the chapter, and indeed of Chapters 7–12, is that expressed by Jesus in John 16:33: 'I have told you these things, so that in me you may have peace. In this world you will have trouble. But take heart! I have overcome the world.' These words were spoken not simply for the disciples in the immediate crisis but for the time after the Resurrection and Pentecost, and indeed for every generation of the faithful until the Lord returns.

---

[16] An exception is the fine series of sermons by James Philip, published as *By the Rivers of Babylon* (Didasko Press, Aberdeen 1971-72).

If we wonder why a mere two verses are given to the mighty Persian and Greek empires, and so much concentration is made on the events which were the background to the rise of Antiochus, we can understand it better from this perspective. The end of the Exile must have seemed to many as the final answer to their prayers: 'When the LORD brought back the captives to Zion, we were like men who dreamed' (Ps. 126:1), and no doubt there were high hopes of great days. However, post-exilic prophets such as Malachi paint a picture of a disillusioned, apathetic community where spiritual fires were burning low. Thus the prophetic word was needed more than ever.

Yet during the Persian empire and the short-lived empire of Alexander, nothing happened which seriously threatened the position of the Jews back in their own land. However, with the emergence of Antiochus another and perhaps worse exile beckoned. That had to be prepared for and faith built up to meet it. Indeed the nature of this chapter, with its using Antiochus as one example of evil, encourages every believer to stand firm until the end of the particular trouble and indeed until the End itself. Prophecy never takes away the need for faith, rather it is given to encourage and strengthen faith.

2. Theologically this chapter is most important. Daniel, we are told, in Chapter 1 continued right into the reign of Cyrus. Here (and more explicitly in 12:3) all who are wise are promised that they will continue. This is because they are given life from God and their conduct is in line with his truth. Only truth has staying power; the nature of human power is to be transitory and insubstantial. We have seen all through the book many insights into the nature of power. This chapter does not, nor do the others, deny the reality of human power, nor as we have also seen is it simply like a puppet show. Political ambition, greed, diplomacy, military conquests, marriage alliances, bribery and flattery all play their part. The individuals and communities concerned all had genuine choices to make and were not obliged to behave in

the way they did. Yet the outworking of the consequences of these actions forms a pattern, as sowing leads to reaping.

3. We are reminded again of the limitations of our knowledge. At the end of the whole vision of which this chapter is part, Daniel says, 'I heard, but I did not understand' (12:8). This should warn us against over-confident interpretation of all the details. Yet some things can be understood. History is not simply raw material for us to construct lessons and philosophies as we will; we need revelation and that revelation is given not to satisfy our curiosity but to help us to look at the world with God's eyes and present the world with God's agenda. We must not forget that this whole revelation arises from Bible study and prayer, and unless these are at the heart of what we do we will not appreciate this great chapter.

4. The aim of all Scripture is to lead us to Christ and it is in the light of Christ that we must see these later chapters of Daniel. This chapter, as we have seen, brings us to the brink of the last days. Rome, as Antiochus discovered to his cost, was the rising power on the world stage and, as we noticed in the commentary on Chapter 7, it was in the time when Rome ruled that the 'Prince of princes' (8:25) came to earth. Thus this teaching is for the last days and is, in the words of 2 Peter 1:19, 'a light shining in a dark place, until the day dawns and the morning star rises in your hearts.'

Questions for further study

1. Is this a necessary chapter?

2. If this is prophecy, how can we reconcile that with human freedom to choose?

3. What are the marks of a godless régime?

12

Those who are wise

In New College, which houses the Divinity Faculty of Edinburgh University, there is a splendid theological library in the part of the college buildings which was once a church. In the basement there is a small chapel commemorating a minister who served there last century. A wall plaque quotes Daniel 12:3 in the King James Version: 'They that be wise shall shine as the brightness of the firmament; and they that turn many to righteousness as the stars for ever and ever.' Many times when I was a student there I found this was a place to go and remember the true priorities of Christian ministry – 'turning many to righteousness'. As the book of Daniel comes to its close it is true priorities which are being underlined in this final chapter.

The chapter falls into two sections: verses 1-4 are the final part of the prophecy which began in 11:2; verses 5-13 are an epilogue both to this section which began in 10:1 and indeed to the book as a whole.

The World to Come (12:1-4)
Chapter 11 ended with the destruction of the antichrist figure and 12:1 continues without a break.

¹'At that time Michael, the great prince who protects your people, will arise. There will be a time of distress such as has not happened from the beginning of nations until then. But at that time your people – everyone whose name is found written in the book – will be delivered.'

That time is the conflict of the last verses of Chapter 11 and to say that it cannot be eschatological, as do some commentators, is mistaken. We have noticed that in verses 40ff. of Chapter 11 the focus shifts from Antiochus to the more sinister figure of which he is only the foreshadowing. Thus, in a manner characteristic of this book, the writer is saying that **Michael, the great prince**, who has protected the faithful at all crises in history, will now defend them in the last great battle.

Michael is mentioned in the Old Testament only by name in Daniel. It is interesting to speculate whether he may be the Angel of the Lord who led Israel at the Exodus (Exod. 14:19) and the Commander of the army of the Lord who met Joshua outside Jericho (Josh. 5:13-15). Was he the mysterious figure in the Blazing Furnace (see commentary on Chapter 3) and indeed the angel in the Lion's Den (Chapter 6)? The New Testament mentions him in two significant passages. Jude describes him as 'the archangel' and speaks of him defending the body of Moses against the devil. This fits well with his role here as protector of God's people. In Revelation 12:7ff. he leads his angels in a successful battle with the dragon and his angels, exactly the kind of role envisaged here in Chapter 12. The fascinating feature of this cosmic battle is that it is the heavenly counterpart of the victory of Christ on the cross over the devil and his angels. Thus the faithful overcome 'by the blood of the Lamb'. The evidence thus points to the rising of Michael being associated with the triumph of Christ and the coming of the kingdom. A further relevant passage is 1 Thessalonians 4:16 where the coming of the Lord is heralded by 'the voice of the archangel'.

Moreover, **the time of distress** of unprecedented severity echoes Jeremiah 30:7: 'How awful that day will be! None will like it.' That referred to the Exile itself, Chapters 8–11 focus on the Antiochus persecution, both of which foreshadow the End time. This is when Michael **will arise** or 'stand over' – the word *amad* is used in many senses. It is clearly related to Michael's activity as advocate in the heavenly court (cp. Satan's role as accuser in Job 1 and 2), but it also means 'come to protect' and suggests comprehensive defence of God's people.

Who are God's people? Here they are those **whose name is found written in the book**. This passage echoes Psalm 69:28

and foreshadows the awesome scene in Revelation 20:11-15
where judgment is determined by whether or not the names of
the dead are found in 'the book of life'. Goldingay, in a felici-
tous phrase, calls this 'the citizen list of the true Jerusalem'.[1]
This is the final answer of Jerusalem to Babylon. The motif of
the books has, of course, already occurred in 7:10: 'The court
was seated and the books were opened.'

But a further question must be faced. What of all these untold
multitudes who have been killed, God's people in all ages who
have died without receiving the spectacular rescues of Chapters
3 and 6? Now follow two of the most glorious verses in the
book, indeed in the entire Old Testament.

> [2]Multitudes who sleep in the dust of the earth will awake: some to
> everlasting life, others to shame and everlasting contempt. [3]Those
> who are wise will shine like the brightness of the heavens, and
> those who lead many to righteousness, like the stars for ever and
> ever.'

All commentators agree that verse 2 refers to bodily resurrection but there are wide differences about its precise significance.
Most take this to be a 'late' idea, unknown in the earlier period,
and thus giving another indication of the second century date of
the book. However, there are a number of things which indicate
that this is not the correct view. The first is that the reference to
the dust of the earth is most probably an echo of Genesis 3:19:
'dust you are and to dust you will return'. Yet it is only a few
verses later that God guards the tree of life in case humans 'eat
and live for ever'. There, already, is the concept of the possibility of eternal life. At the moment of greatest hopelessness, when
the future of humans seems to be to go down into the dust of
death, we are reminded that the Creator formed man out of that
same dust; what he did once he can do again. Thus Daniel is
pointing us forward to a new creation.

Further, some have argued that, since the word **multitudes**

[1] Goldingay, p. 306.

rather than 'everyone' is used, a more limited number such as the Maccabaean martyrs is intended. However, Baldwin is almost certainly right when she argues: 'The emphasis is not upon many as opposed to all, but rather on the numbers involved.'[2] The passage is echoed in John 5:28:29 where Jesus says: 'all who are in their graves will hear his voice and come out – those who have done good will rise to live and those who have done evil will rise to be condemned.' What is envisaged there, and here in the Daniel passage, is a general resurrection on the Last Day.

It is also important to realise that much of the accepted wisdom about the absence of any idea of life after death in the Old Testament is built on a misunderstanding of the type of literature in which many of the statements occur. There are many passages in Job which deny the possibility of a life beyond the grave: for example, 'As a cloud vanishes and is gone, so he who goes down to the grave does not return' (7:9); 'so man lies down and does not rise; till the heavens are no more, men will not awake or be roused from their sleep' (14:12); 'only a few years will pass before I go on the journey of no return' (16:22). What must be realised is that these are dramatic, not theological, statements. Job, in his agony, feels like that, but that does not represent the reality of the situation. Similarly when we read in Ecclesiastes 3:19-20: 'Man's fate is like that of the animals; the same fate awaits them both .... All go to the same place; all come from dust, and to dust all return', we must remember the perspective of the author. He is writing about life 'under the sun', giving us a clear and unforgettable picture of existence without God. Thus we have a cold realism; all life does end, no one comes back; there is mystery and silence.

By contrast what we have here in Daniel is revelation; this is the final part of this long and impressive speech by the heavenly visitor of Chapter 10 and thus, like all of the speech, is a glimpse of reality. However, we must not regard this as 'the only generally accepted reference to resurrection in the Hebrew Bible'.[3] It is true that the term 'everlasting life' probably occurs first here,

---

[2] Baldwin, p. 204.   [3] Collins, p. 392.

but the idea of the presence of the Lord continuing after death is frequent in the Psalter: for example, 'eternal pleasures at your right hand' (16:11); 'I shall see your face; when I awake, I shall be satisfied with seeing your likeness' (17:15); 'You guide me with your counsel, and afterwards you will take me into glory' (73:24).[4] Obviously a full belief in the life beyond the grave waits until the Resurrection but there is no doubt that the faith of the Old Testament has a clear eschatological perspective too often ignored or denied. The author of Hebrews emphasises this: 'They did not receive the things promised; they only saw them and welcomed them from a distance' (11:13). Their faith looked to the heavenly city.

Not only does verse 2 clearly point to a resurrection but equally clearly it envisages two different destinies. The destiny of the faithful is to be developed in verse 3, but the destiny of the wicked is to be **shame and everlasting contempt**. No details are given but it is worth noting that this verse implies conscious continuance of life beyond the grave for both righteous and wicked and thus does not fit well with 'Annihilationism' which has become increasingly popular, including in evangelical circles.

Verse 3 goes on to say something of the destiny of the wise. The wise are those who live their lives and govern what they say in harmony with the purposes for which God created the world. 11:33 has spoken of how they instruct others which is clearly equivalent to 'leading many to righteousness'. The so-called Wisdom books – Proverbs, Ecclesiastes and Job – explore and submit to rigorous questioning that whole world-view. But in this book the supreme example of wisdom is Daniel himself, along with his three friends. 1:17 has spoken of how God endowed these four young men with wisdom and this was to carry them all to positions of great eminence and influence.

---

[4] M. Dahood in *Psalms* (Anchor Bible, 3 Vols. 1966-70) argues very strongly on the basis of such passages for a belief in an after-life. He regards these psalms as very ancient, drawing attention to parallels in ancient Canaanite poetry.

Similarly 2:21 speaks of God who 'gives wisdom to the wise'. Here now we are given a glimpse of their final destiny. This destiny is not mere survival but to share in the glory of heaven, to be a prominent part of that kingdom which will never be overthrown.

The language used deliberately links the wise with the Creator and more particularly the heavenly court. The court of heaven and the angels are associated with creation in Job 38:7 where, when God created the world, 'the morning stars sang together and all the sons of God shouted for joy'. They have shone like stars in the darkness of the world and so they will shine even more brightly in the world to come. Here is a powerful motive for evangelism. The **leading many to righteousness** anticipates in this world the life of the world to come and gives renewed energy to work for the coming of the kingdom.

The long final revelation is now at an end but before the final scene in the book the heavenly messenger has a further instruction for Daniel:

> 4"But you, Daniel, close up and seal the words of the scroll until the time of the end. Many will go here and there to increase knowledge.'

Here is another indication that the book of Daniel speaks beyond its own time and indeed is particularly addressed to 'the last days', the time between the comings of Christ. **Seal** has both the meaning of 'keep safe' and also 'demonstrate authenticity'. Similarly Isaiah 8:16 speaks of the need to 'Bind up the testimony and seal up the law among my disciples'. In many ways it is a development of 'leading many to righteousness'. Long after Daniel's day, as his words are not only kept but taught, multitudes will hear and respond. We find the same idea in Paul's charge to Timothy: 'Entrust to reliable men who will also be qualified to teach others' (2 Tim. 2:2). Only at the time of the end would the true meaning of these revelations emerge. Here we must remember the 'now' and 'not yet' of the kingdom. Since the Son of Man has already come, much is clear which was only glimpsed by Daniel, but until the Son of Man comes again in the clouds of heaven much remains mystery.

Yet there is enough revelation to bring salvation, enough light to live by, and enough knowledge to guide our footsteps safely. But in spite of this many will persist in looking for enlightenment in the wrong places. The latter part of verse 4 probably echoes Amos 8:12: 'Men will stagger from sea to sea and wander from north to east, searching for the word of the LORD, but they will not find it.' Much earlier in the book of Daniel we have seen the abject failure of magicians, sorcerers et al to impart knowledge and wisdom. Revelation, which comes by the Word of God, is necessary for true understanding.

Epilogue (12:5-13)

This final scene takes place at the river where this last great revelation has been given. Once again it is not entirely clear how many figures are in the scene. And once again there are questions to be asked:

> ⁵Then I, Daniel, looked, and there before me stood two others, one on this bank of the river and one on the opposite bank. ⁶One of them said to the man clothed in linen, who was above the waters of the river, 'How long will it be before these astonishing things are fulfilled?'

The **astonishing things** are the events of 11:2–12:3 and the question echoes that asked by 'a holy one' in 8:13. Even the heavenly court does not have perfect knowledge of events yet to unfold. A similar emphasis occurs in 1 Peter 1:12: 'Even angels long to look into these things.'

However, we are left in no doubt about the importance of these matters by the next verse:

> ⁷The man clothed in linen, who was above the waters of the river, lifted his right hand and his left hand towards heaven, and I heard him swear by him who lives for ever, saying, 'It will be for a time,

times and half a time. When the power of the holy people has been finally broken, all these things will be completed.'

It was normal practice to raise one hand at the swearing of an oath (see e.g. Gen. 14:22; Exod. 6:8; Ezek. 20:5), but to raise two hands suggests something unusually significant. Perhaps the most striking parallel is Deuteronomy 32:40: 'I lift my hand to heaven and declare: As surely as I live for ever ...' These words were spoken by the Lord himself at the end of the Exodus journey just before the people entered the promised land. Now at the end of the Exile, as significant events are again happening – which, as we have seen, foreshadow even more significant events – **who lives forever** is a reminder of the theology of the book; all these events are conditioned by time but only the One who lives for ever can have a kingdom that will never end. He alone is the guarantor that this revelation will be fulfilled.

Once again the mysterious **time, times and half a time**, first encountered in 7:25, is mentioned. There we were told that the saints would be 'handed over' to the fourth beast for a time, but that at the end of it the heavenly court would sit and the Most High would reign, and his people would reign with him for ever. This is one of the many links which bind the apocalyptic part of the book together. The **holy people** is also a phrase reminiscent of Deuteronomy (e.g. 7:6; 14:2) and a reminder of the continuity of God's people throughout the ages. Not even the most devastating of circumstances is outside God's control. Just before the Exodus, again at the Exile, and again in the time of Antiochus, evil seemed to triumph; but the Most High reigns.

Daniel is still bewildered and asks a somewhat different question:

> [8]I heard, but I did not understand. So I asked, 'My lord, what will the outcome of all this be?'

This is another reminder that even after revelation has been received there is still need for faith. The further answer given to him is also one of mystery; there will always, in this world, be unanswered questions which we have to live with.

⁹He replied, 'Go your way, Daniel, because the words are closed up and sealed until the time of the end. ¹⁰Many will be purified, made spotless and refined, but the wicked will continue to be wicked. None of the wicked will understand, but those who are wise will understand.

¹¹From the time that the daily sacrifice is abolished and the abomination that causes desolation is set up, there will be 1,290 days. ¹²Blessed is the one who waits for and reaches the end of the 1,335 days.'

The purpose of receiving revelation and leading many to righteousness is to strengthen faith and help people to endure to the end. There will always be great temptation to give up in the face of persecution or adversity, but all this opposition has an end in view, that of refining and purifying. This same emphasis is to be found in the Letter to the Hebrews, perhaps the part of the New Testament which more than any other emphasizes the importance of persevering: 'No discipline seems pleasant at the time, but painful. Later on, however, it produces a harvest of righteousness and peace for those who have been trained by it' (12:11). The wicked persist in their course, an idea echoed in Revelation 22:11: 'Let him who does wrong continue to do wrong; let him who is vile continue to be vile.' This is, of course, exemplified by Antiochus and, earlier in the book, by Belshazzar. As we have already seen, this does not mean they were puppets driven headlong by an inexorable fate; rather that they made choices which gradually hardened into an inexorable anti-God attitude and thus a destiny of judgment.

Verse 11 has caused a lot of trouble to some commentators because of the two different times given and the difficulty of fitting these into an historical context. Many take it to mean the period between the removal of the burnt offering by Antiochus and either the rededication of the Temple or the death of Antiochus. It is further argued that we are given two dates because the second century writer or an editor realised that the End had not come when the first period elapsed and thus revised the date (which on that interpretation also came and went with nothing remarkable happening). When, however, we realise that Exile, Antiochus, Romans *et al* were all simply anticipations of the final end the matter becomes clearer.

Much mystery remains but two things can be said. The first is that times and seasons belong to God. He knows exactly how long kingdoms and rulers will last and he is not taken by surprise. Times of distress and persecution will not go on forever. The second is a call to perseverance. The period of the End, the time between the Comings of Christ, variously called 'a time, times and half a time' or given numbers of days (as here and in 8:14), will be a long time in human terms. This is true for the whole Church throughout the ages as well as for individual believers in their time. Thus there is need to keep on going when the trouble extends beyond what was originally expected, when it lasts for 1,335 days instead of 1,290 days. This is the emphasis of Jesus' apocalyptic discourse in Mark 13. Verse 7 of that chapter speaks of 'the end is still to come' and verse 13 speaks of the need to endure to the end. A similar thread runs through the apocalyptic parables in Matthew 24 and 25 where again the importance of perseverance and watchfulness is underlined; there the wise servant continues his work although the master delays, while the wicked servant works against him (24:47-51; 25:14-30).

In this book the supreme example of the wise servant who has 'remained' (1:21) is, of course, Daniel himself, and as the book closes we are reminded of his faithfulness and endurance and look beyond to his promised reward:

> [13]'As for you, go your way till the end. You will rest, and then at the end of the days you will rise to receive your allotted inheritance.'

This verse finely illustrates the habitual emphasis of biblical eschatology. This always has two sides: the first is to live faithfully in the present and the second is the promise of future reward. **Go your way** is a reminder that, old as he is, Daniel's earthly life is to be lived for God until the very end. **You will rest** probably echoes Isaiah 57:2: 'Those who walk uprightly enter into peace; they find rest as they lie in death.' This suggests that he will soon die; after all by now he is a very old man. However, that is temporary. He is to be one of the wise of verses 2 and 3 who will be raised to be part of an eternal and glorious kingdom.

This is well expressed in the following benediction:

> Now to God Almighty, whose plans for us do not end in death, to our Lord Jesus Christ, who entered our world so that we might enter his, and to the Holy Spirit, who works in our hearts constantly preparing us for that great day, be all our praise and love until we meet him face to face. Amen.[5]

General Comments

It would be useful to draw together some of the threads not just of this final chapter but of the book as a whole by reflecting on the main themes of Daniel. As we have seen, the specific situation of the Exile, and beyond that the Maccabaean period, raised huge questions about the nature of God, the riddle of events and the apparent failure of God's kingdom. There are six issues I would like to comment on.

1. The Nature of God

What kind of God is it who allowed his city, temple and nation to be destroyed? Part of the answer is suggested by Isaiah 45:15: 'Truly you are a God who hides himself, a God and Saviour of Israel.' For much of this book God is hidden, occasionally making dramatic appearances such as Chapters 3, 5 and 6. However, much of the book reflects the apparent absence of God, which so often is the experience of the believer in the world. There is a striking parallel with the book of Esther where even God's name is not mentioned.

Yet this hiddenness is a very different thing from absence.

---

[5] Quoted in *Still Waters, Deep Waters* (Albatross 1987), p. 203.

From the very beginning the Exile is seen as under the Lord's control. We noticed the use of the verb 'give' which demonstrates his control over human history. This is developed in 2:20-23 where God is the one who 'changes times and seasons ... sets up kings and deposes them'. This emphasis runs through the apocalyptic chapters, particularly Chapter 7, and is acknowledged by Nebuchadnezzar (2:47; 4:2-3, 34-35) and by Darius (6:26-27).

This, of course, exists side by side with the fact that he is the Lord of the Covenant with whom humans can have a relationship. Much of the book gives us an insight into Daniel's walk with God, and the importance of his Word and prayer are underlined again and again. The God of Daniel in fact echoes the pictures of God in Genesis 1 and 2; in Chapter 1 the transcendent Creator who makes all there is by his powerful Word and in Chapter 2 the God who comes down and takes clay. This points to the day when God will appear in the Lord Jesus Christ, one with him and one of us.

2. The Kingdom of God

This theme is a natural implication of the nature of God, i.e. how is his rule to be exercised in the world. One common theme of the book is that human power is not always bad and that even under pagan monarchs good things can happen. This is seen, for example, in the power and influence Daniel and his friends are given at court. Yet human power, especially represented by the Fourth Beast and Antiochus, can have a devilish aspect and challenge God himself.

Daniel shows the 'now' and 'not yet' aspects of the kingdom of God. Already in the godly lives of Daniel and his friends we have glimpses of another kind of kingdom. Similarly the dramatic events of Chapters 3, 5 and 6 show the life of the world to come breaking into this one. Similarly the apocalyptic chapters begin with the throne of the Eternal God towering over the passing human régimes. Glimpses of the kingdom help the believer to live *now* in the light of *then*. However, the kingdom will only finally arrive when the Son of Man comes in the clouds of heaven to establish righteousness and peace.

3. The Nature of Revelation

One of the most striking features of Daniel is the variety of literary genres employed. Story is prominent in Chapters 1–6 but we also have dream, vision and prayers. The apocalyptic part includes detailed visions, heavenly conversations, prophecy and reflection. This is a reminder that the whole Bible itself uses a multitude of literary forms to convey the truth of God and to suggest something of his many-sided glory.

A number of considerations flow from this. The first is that our whole personality, including our imagination, needs to be engaged if we are to respond to God. It is instructive to see the ways in which Daniel responds to the visions and messages: 'I ... was deeply troubled by my thoughts, and my face turned pale' (7:28); 'I was terrified and fell prostrate' (8.17); 'I was appalled by the vision' (8:27); 'I ... pleaded ... in fasting, and in sackcloth and ashes' (9:3); various verses in Chapter 10: 'mourned' (v. 2), 'deathly pale' (v. 8), 'trembling' (v. 11), 'overcome with anguish' (v. 16); 'I did not understand' (12:8). These, and similar verses, show how awesome and demanding it is to receive divine revelation.

This does not encourage an unbalanced and vague mysticism. Such phrases as 'know and understand' (9:25) and 'set your mind to gain understanding' (10:12) show that while we cannot understand everything it does not mean that we cannot understand anything. Moreover, as the last verse of Chapter 12 demonstrates, the aim of revelation is a practical one – to help the believer to live in the present.

But most importantly, in every case where there is a vision, in Chapters 2 and 4 as well as in the apocalyptic chapters, the pictures are always explained by the words. In Chapters 1–6 Daniel himself is given authoritative words which explain the dreams of Chapters 2 and 4 and the writing on the wall of Chapter 5. In Chapters 7–12 the heavenly messengers give messages to

Daniel himself. It is because of the word from heaven that we have the light shining in a dark place.

4. The Nature of Reality

The book of Daniel is unique among apocalyptic writings in that the main character is pictured as living in the real world of people and events. Books such as 1 Enoch do indeed have stories but these happen in the supernatural world. Daniel lives his life in this world because he is in touch with another world which is ultimately more real and substantial than the world of politics and human power.

Thus the book moves on these two levels and, as we have seen, only those in touch with the world to come can truly influence this world. Especially in Chapter 10 we have seen the spiritual powers which govern life here and the way that only prayer can be effective.

5. The Life of Faith

For the believer, living in this world will always be tough and the end of one Exile will not mean the end of difficulties. Sometimes this will take the form of flattery and glittering prizes as in much of Chapters 1–6; many times it will be savage persecution as in Chapters 3–6 and much of Chapters 7–12. Sometimes this persecution will be intense and prolonged (e.g. 12:1) and rescue appear to be delayed (e.g. 12:12).

Daniel himself (and his friends) are a model of how to live in a pagan society. We noticed his courtesy and flexibility in Chapter 1, uncompromising on principle but pragmatic and co-operative on details. Similarly, Daniel and his friends play an active and constructive part in the government, in Daniel's case at least during the whole Exilic period. Yet Daniel's real centre of gravity was his prayer life. Chapters 2, 6 and 9 especially focus on the power and effectiveness of Daniel's prayers. It is the realisation of the nature of God, his kingdom, and the nature of revelation and reality, which are the heart of Daniel's prayers and gives them their depth and influence.

6. Eschatology

Daniel is a book for the last days. The central vision of the Son of Man coming with the clouds of heaven (7:13) points to the climax of history, and the chapters which follow unfold the con- flicts which continue between the comings of Christ and will end only when the powers of evil are finally destroyed. One or two things call for comment.

The first is that in Daniel we reach the time when Jerusalem and Babylon are not simply literal cities but represent the great realities of the cities of God and of the world. Jerusalem/Zion is the people of God, the city which is also the Bride (see Revelation 20–21). Babylon is the city of the world doomed to destruction (see Revelation 18–19). Living in one city while looking for and travelling to another is one of the great themes of the Bible (see its use in Hebrews 11). The coming of Christ already has given the death blow to Babylon; but until he comes again living in Babylon will be a reality for the believer, and so the book of Daniel is particularly relevant.

Thus the book of Daniel impels us beyond itself and focuses on the future when the everlasting kingdom will finally be established and the Lord Jesus Christ, who is the ultimate fulfilment of the book, will return. Thus as we come to the end of the book we echo the great prayer of the early Church: 'Maranatha. Come Lord Jesus.'

Questions for further study

1. Who are the wise?

2. What is the chapter saying about godly living?

3. What light does this chapter throw on life after death?

Index of Main Themes

Also by Christian Focus

How God Treats His Friends

Robert Fyall

What are we do do or say when a genuinely good person is overwhelmed by appalling disasters? Such a character was Job – a man who was wise, compassionate and historic, yet who suffered desperate tragedy. Such situations raise many questions, questions such as:

Why does God allow it to happen?
What is the devil's role in the problem?
Does human sin result in divine judgments?

These and other questions are dealt with by Robert Fyall.

ISBN 1 85792 115 1   pocket paperback   160 pages

Below is the foreword by Sinclair Ferguson (Westminster Theological Seminary, Philadelphia) to *How God Treats His Friends?*

I have sometimes thought that it is one of the great 'treats' of life in the Christian church to have friends who combine special expertise in the study of the Old Testament with a commitment to share its riches. To read, or to listen to exposition which is sensitive to its literature, language, imagery and themes is a high privilege. It is to have the mind stretched to take in the sheer greatness of the covenant-making God, to have the will redirected to serve him, and, yes, to have the emotions cleansed. Those – like Robert Fyall – who are able to handle the Old Testament with such skill are among the treasures of the church.

Dr Fyall is an Old Testament scholar who currently teaches at St John's College, Durham and brings to his writing his considerable scholarly expertise. But more than that, in these pages he places his gifts at the disposal of non-experts like ourselves, and invites us to read through the Book of Job with him, as friends. As we do so, we will soon feel that he is sitting beside us and – as a patient teacher – is pointing out many of the things he knows we need to learn, and asking us, 'Do you see this? And this? And this?' One indication of Robert Fyall's gifts is that when *he* points things out to you, they become hard to miss!

I think I can promise you that the experience of reading *How God Treats His Friends* will be very rewarding indeed. In his easy and pleasant style Dr Fyall will show you wisdom, insight, pathos, challenge and encouragement – and all from one priceless book of the Bible.

The Book of Job is a majestic piece of literature by any standard. But it is more; it is God's word, and with the help of these chapters you will at times be stunned by its power and find it speaking to you in a multitude of fresh ways.

How God Treats His Friends has many fine points. Perhaps the most important of them is that its interpretation of the Book of Job is consistent and convincing. It would be wrong to steal a book's thunder, but perhaps it will whet your appetite to know that, unlike many commentaries and studies of Job, Dr Fyall's exposition persuasively interprets it from beginning to end. Those who have read other works on Job may well find themselves saying as they come to the conclusion of this one, '*Now* it is clear what the Book of Job is about; it all makes sense; why didn't I see that before?'.

A further strength should be mentioned. As someone whose interests lie in the world of the ancient Near East in which the Old Testament is set, Dr Fyall is sensitive to the ideas, beliefs and concepts which were part of that paganly religious environment. He shows how the Book of Job, like other biblical books, used the language and concepts of its day in the service of divine revelation. To some readers of the Old Testament this may be a new and strange concept to grasp. But in many ways it will underline the sheer power with which 'In the past God spoke to our forefathers' (Hebrews 1:1). The marvellous thing is that Robert Fyall deals with all this in a way that demonstrates how Scripture speaks to our own time, and indeed to our own needs too.

These qualities alone would make *How God Treats His Friends* a must-buy. Careful biblical interpretation at its best is worth reading for its own sake. But add to this pearls of wisdom (dropped, it seems, almost in passing) which help us to study the Bible better for ourselves, as well as insights which will help us to live the Christian life more consistently – and here you have a book of great value.

'No-one who reads the Book of Job can remain indifferent; it is an exhilarating if often bruising experience', writes Dr Fyall. So, prepare to be bruised and exhilarated as you turn these pages with your Bible beside you. As you read you will come to appreciate the Book of Job in a new way; you will also want to read the Old Testament much more. And I suspect you will be on the look-out for another book from the same author. But until then, *How God Treats His Friends* will be worth re-reading!

Focus on the Bible Commentaries

Exodus – John L. Mackay*
Deuteronomy – Alan Harman
Judges and Ruth – Stephen Dray
1 and 2 Samuel – David Searle*
1 and 2 Kings – Robert Fyall*
Proverbs – Eric Lane (late 1998)
Daniel – Robert Fyall (1998)
Hosea – Michael Eaton
Amos – O Palmer Robertson*
Jonah-Zephaniah – John L. Mackay
Haggai-Malachi – John L. Mackay
Matthew – Charles Price (1998)
Mark – Geoffrey Grogan
John – Steve Motyer (1999)
Romans – R. C. Sproul
2 Corinthians – Geoffrey Grogan
Galatians – Joseph Pipa*
Ephesians – R. C. Sproul
Philippians – Hywel Jones
1 and 2 Thessalonians – Richard Mayhue (1999)
The Pastoral Epistles – Douglas Milne
Hebrews – Walter Riggans (1998)
James – Derek Prime
1 Peter – Derek Cleave
2 Peter – Paul Gardner (1998)
Jude – Paul Gardner

Journey Through the Old Testament – Bill Cotton
How To Interpret the Bible – Richard Mayhue

Those marked with an * are currently being written.

MENTOR TITLES

Creation and Change by Douglas Kelly (large format, 272 pages)
A scholarly defence of the literal seven-day account of the creation of all things as detailed in Genesis 1. The author is Professor of Systematic Theology in Reformed Theological Seminary in Charlotte, North Carolina, USA.

The Healing Promise by Richard Mayhue (large format, 288 pages)
A clear biblical examination of the claims of Health and Wealth preachers. The author is Dean of The Master's Seminary, Los Angeles, California.

Puritan Profiles by William Barker (hardback, 320 pages)
The author is Professor of Church History at Westminster Theological Seminary, Philadelphia, USA. In this book he gives biographical profiles of 54 leading Puritans, most of whom were involved in the framing of the Westminster Confession of Faith.

Creeds, Councils and Christ by Gerald Bray (large format, 224 pages)
The author, who teaches at Samford University, Birmingham, Alabama, explains the historical circumstances and doctrinal differences that caused the early church to frame its creeds. He argues that a proper appreciation of the creeds will help the confused church of today.

MENTOR COMMENTARIES

1 and 2 Chronicles by Richard Pratt (hardback, 520 pages)
The author is professor of Old Testament at Reformed Theological Seminary, Orlando, USA. In this commentary he gives attention to the structure of Chronicles as well as the Chronicler's reasons for his different emphases from that of 1 and 2 Kings.

Psalms by Alan Harman (hardback, 420 pages)
The author, now retired from his position as a professor of Old Testament, lives in Australia. His commentary includes a comprehensive introduction to the psalms as well as a commentary on each psalm.

Amos by Gray Smith (hardback, 320 pages)
Gary Smith, a professor of Old Testament in Bethel Seminary, Minneapolis, USA, exegetes the text of Amos by considering issues of textual criticism, structure, historical and literary background, and the theological significance of the book.

Reformed Theological Writings
R. A. Finlayson

This volume contains a selection of doctrinal studies, divided into three sections:

General theology
The God of Israel; God In Three Persons; God the Father; The Person of Christ; The Love of the Spirit in Man's Redemption; The Holy Spirit in the Life of Christ; The Messianic Psalms; The Terminology of the Atonement; The Ascension; The Holy Spirit in the Life of the Christian; The Assurance of Faith; The Holy Spirit in the Life of the Church; The Church – The Body of Christ; The Authority of the Church; The Church in Augustine; Disruption Principles; The Reformed Doctrine of the Sacraments; The Theology of the Lord's Day, The Christian Sabbath; The Last Things.

Issues Facing Evangelicals
Christianity and Humanism; How Liberal Theology Infected Scotland; Neo-Orthodoxy; Neo-Liberalism and Neo-Fundamentalism; The Ecumenical Movement; Modern Theology and the Christian Message.

The Westminster Confession of Faith
The Significance of the Westminster Confession; The Doctrine of Scripture in the Westminster Confession of Faith; The Doctrine of God in the Westminster Confession of Faith; Particular Redemption in the Westminster Confession of Faith; Efficacious Grace in the Westminster Confession of Faith; Predestination in the Westminster Confession of Faith; The Doctrine of Man in the Westminster Confession of Faith.

R. A. Finlayson was for many years the leading theologian of the Free Church of Scotland and one of the most effective preachers and speakers of his time; those who were students in the 1950s deeply appreciated his visits to Christian Unions and IVF conferences. This volume contains posthumously edited theological lectures which illustrate his brilliant gift for simple, logical and yet warm-hearted presentation of Christian doctrine (I Howard Marshall).

272 pages   ISBN 1 85792 259 X   large format

Books by Donald Bridge

JESUS - THE MAN AND HIS MESSAGE

What impact did Jesus make on the circumstances and culture of his time? What is it about him that identifies him both as a unique Saviour and the greatest example of gospel communication?

Donald Bridge challenges the way we view Jesus, and our portrayal of him to the world around us. He argues that walking with Jesus today means reading his words, welcoming the impact of his personality, embracing the provision he makes for us, and sharing his good news with others.

Donald Bridge combines a lifetime of study of the Gospels with an intimate knowledge of the land where Jesus lived and taught. He has been both an evangelist and a pastor, as well as working for several years in the Garden Tomb, Jerusalem.

176 PAGES   B FORMAT

ISBN 1 85792 117 8

SPIRITUAL GIFTS AND THE CHURCH
Donald Bridge and David Phypers

First published in the 1970s, when the Charismatic Movement became prominent in British church life, this classic study of gifts, the individual and the church has been revised and expanded in light of developments since then. The authors, Donald Bridge and David Phypers, give a balanced view of a difficult and controversial issue.

The baptism of the Spirit, with its associated gifts, is a subject which has perplexed and fascinated Christians. It is unfortunately one which also divides Christians who disagree over the extent to which gifts should appear in the Church.

Donald Bridge is an evangelist and church consultant and David Phypers is a Church of England pastor.

192 PAGES   B FORMAT

ISBN 1 85792 141 0

Christian Focus Publications publishes biblically-accurate books for adults and children. The books in the adult range are published in three imprints.

Christian Heritage contains classic writings from the past.

Christian Focus contains popular works including biographies, commentaries, doctrine, and Christian living.

Mentor focuses on books written at a level suitable for Bible College and seminary students, pastors, and others; the imprint includes commentaries, doctrinal studies, examination of current issues, and church history.

For a free catalogue of all our titles, please write to
Christian Focus Publications,
Geanies House, Fearn,
Ross-shire, IV20 1TW, Great Britain

For details of our titles visit us on our web site
http://www.geanies.org.uk/cfp